Contents

Note: *Philadelphia, Here I Come!* is divided into three Episodes. Episode Three is subdivided into two parts. For the purposes of this commentary, the dramatic events have been isolated and analysed separately, while the original sequence of the play's format has of course been maintained. This is an artificial breakdown but one which should facilitate the student in understanding the play as a whole. All references to the play are taken from *Philadelphia, Here I Come!* (London, Faber and Faber, 1965).

Analysis and Commentary

EPISODE 1

Introducing Gar, Madge and S.B.

It is the night before Gar's departure for Philadelphia. 'He is ecstatic with joy and excitement', and he sings and waltzes around the kitchen. He forces Madge, the housekeeper, to do a few steps as he cavorts around. The time is ten past seven. We learn that on his last day in his father's grocery business, Gar has worked ten minutes overtime. When Madge goes off to the scullery, we are introduced to Private. Through Private we enter the world of Gar's inner thoughts. He fantasises about being a pilot, a star footballer and a soldier. Madge interrupts his fantasies and their conversation prepares us for the entrance of Gar's father, S.B. When S.B. appears, he questions his son about the coils of barbed wire which came in on the mail-van. We note Public's and Private's reaction to the conversation. (pp. 15-21)

COMMENTARY

THIS opening sequence conveys much information about the main characters and the relationship between them. We find Gar in an exuberant mood. Tomorrow he will be free — away from the small village of Ballybeg, away from the shop, away from his friends, and most importantly, away from his father. However, we soon discover that this exuberance is slightly feigned. Gar's 'eejiting' and horseplay with Madge is tinged with a search for affection ('Will you miss me?'). Having extracted 'I will — I will — I will — I —' from Madge, his thoughts turn to his father.

S.B. O'Donnell has given no indication that this is a special day. Instead of saying: 'Gar, my son, since you are leaving me forever, you may have the entire day free', S.B. has given him extra work. 'At six o'clock,' Gar tells Madge, 'he remembered about the bloody pollock, and him in the middle of the Angelus *(Stands in imitation of the Father: head bowed, hands on chest. In flat tones —)* "Behold-the-handmaid-of-the-Lord-Gut-and-salt-them-fish."' Gar hides his disappointment and completes his chores with exaggerated gusto ('I lashed so much salt on those bloody fish that any poor bugger that eats them will die of thirst').

The lines that mark the entrance of Private have a crucial significance:

> Public: It's all over.
> Private: *(Off, in echo-chamber voice)* And it's all about to
>   begin. It's all over.
> Public: And it's all about to begin.

At a superficial level, these lines simply mean that Gar's life in Ballybeg is over and his new life in Philadelphia is about to begin. But *Philadelphia, Here I Come!* is not a conventional play with a beginning, a middle and an end. The development of the 'plot' occurs in Gar's mind. The outward physical actions are secondary to the conflict and turmoil of his inner thoughts. Private is the voice of these inner thoughts and through the exchanges of Public and Private, the past experiences, present feelings and future fantasies of Gar are revealed.

The significance of the initial exchange between Public ('It's all over') and Private ('And it's all about to begin') is encapsulated in Madge's prophecy:

> When the boss was his *(Gar's)* age, he was the very same as him: leppin' and eejitin' about and actin' the clown; as like as two peas. And when he's *(Gar)* the age the boss is now, he'll turn out just the same. And although I won't be here to see it, you'll find that he's learned nothin' in-between times. That's people for you — (p. 109)

Gar's attempt to escape from his destiny is doomed to failure, according to Madge; he will end up just like his father; there will be no progress.

From the beginning Private, Gar's alter ego, engrosses the audience with comical fantasies and humorous exchanges with Public. The element of comedy is enhanced by the antics of Public on the stage: he mimics Private's fantasies. The ease with which he changes from one outlandish scenario to another contributes to the aggressively paced opening of Episode 1. Friel believed that the playwright's first function was 'to entertain, to have audiences enjoy themselves, to move them emotionally, to make them laugh and cry and gasp and hold their breath and sit on the edge of their seats'. In *Philadelphia*, Private is the vehicle through which Friel captivates his audience.

At first, one might assume that Private is simply the embodiment of the fun and laughter of Gar's personality. However, when Madge interrupts the Walter Mitty-like fantasies and asks: 'He's said nothing since, I suppose?' (p. 19), referring to S.B.'s silence about Gar's departure, we discover that Private's wit has got a sting in the tail. Outwardly, Gar replies matter-of-factly: 'Not a word'; inwardly his private self replies: 'The bugger'. This is the first articulation of the vehement emotion Gar feels towards his father. While Public maintains a stoical attitude towards S.B.'s lack of reaction— ('it's a matter of total indifference to me'), Private is seething with anger and frustration: 'What the hell do you care about him. Screwballs! Skinflint! Skittery Face! You're free of him and his stinking bloody shop.' (p. 20).

With the entrance of S.B. O'Donnell we are introduced to one of the 'establishment' characters of Ballybeg. Like Senator Doogan, Master Boyle, and Canon O'Byrne, S.B. has been assigned a 'title' by Brian Friel. We are told that he is a County Councillor and he is described as a 'responsible, respectable citizen'. But as the character of each of these 'titled' people is developed in the play, the aura of respectability is gradually eroded. Master Boyle is an alcoholic and a failed poet; Senator Doogan is a social snob who feels that his daughter should marry into society rather than for love; Canon O'Byrne is ineffective as a counsellor and fails to translate the communication problems of Gar and S.B. into Christian terms; S.B. is incapable of displaying affection or of communicating with his son. Gar's impressions of these men undermine their image of responsibility and respectability and it may be said that Friel's portrayal of the 'titled' men of Ballybeg is an ironic one. He looks on them as the 'rulers', whose authority is built on a shaky foundation:

> The world, according to the dramatists, is divided into two
> categories. There are the rulers — the establishment — who
> pretend to believe in a traditional social structure that is
> Christian in origin, that is now seen to be false, but which

they still pretend to believe in in order to give them the authority they require. And there are simply the rest — individuals, isolated, separated, sick and disillusioned with their inheritance, existing in the void created by their rejection, waiting without hope for a new social structure that will give a meaning to their lives. (Brian Friel 'The Theatre of Hope and Despair')

When Gar is summoned by his father, 'he assumes in speech and gesture a surly, taciturn gruffness'. He is hesitant and unsure in replying to S.B.'s questions about the barbed wire and inwardly he rebukes himself for being so stupid. However, the self-recriminations are quickly forgotten as S.B. retires to the shop, and soon fantasies of Gar's future in America come to the fore.

Gar's fantasies continue

stage intersection

When S.B. leaves the kitchen, Gar indulges in fantasy again. He 'becomes' a cowboy, the future president of a chain of hotels, a conductor of an orchestra and a violin soloist. (pp. 21-4)

COMMENTARY

GAR is twenty-five years of age, but the tone and content of his private fantasies suggest a mind that is immature and juvenile. He has not yet outgrown the adolescent stage of development. His fantasies are totally unrealistic and they reflect a lack of maturity and an inability to plan adequately for the future. S.B.'s two or three coils of barbed-wire are quickly rejected in Gar's dream world; they will not enclose the vast plains roamed by 'Garry the Kid'! Nor will the future president of the biggest hotel chain in the world be concerned with such trivia!

The make-believe interview for his job in the hotel uncovers information about Gar's past. He spent a year in Dublin at university but failed to sit his First Arts exam. We can infer that his 'pilgrimage' to Harold's Cross had little to do with religion. During his 'several nights in devout prayer' he came to realise that a life of scholarship was not for him, so he returned to his father's business.

Gar is sufficiently clearsighted to recognise Master Boyle as an image of what he himself might become if he chooses to remain in Ballybeg. The example of a schoolmaster whose life is empty except for his drink, his rows with the Canon, and his hopeless plans for the future, may explain in some way why Gar abandoned a life of scholarship and decided to leave his hometown. Gar has had one chance to break away from the narrow confines of Ballybeg: a degree could have offered him a more attractive future than a job in his father's grocery business. But he failed to take advantage of that chance. One wonders if he will make a better effort in his latest bid for freedom.

Gar breaks off his 'mock interview' fantasy by quoting the opening lines of Edmund Burke's *Reflections on the Revolution in France:*

> It is now sixteen or seventeen years since I saw the Queen of France, then the Dauphiness, at Versailles —'

Gar uses this quotation intermittently throughout the play, to break out of fantasy, or to cloud out memories from his mind. It is interesting to speculate on possible reasons for Friel's choice of this material.

Edmund Burke was politically conservative and his view of the French Monarchy was an idealised one — a recreation of a past that may never really have existed. His motive in writing *Reflections* was to discredit the contemporary radical politics of the French Revolution. Burke's idealised past causes him to make a judgement on an inglorious present.

Gar uses the memory of the past in the same way. His past calls into question the present. His memory of his mother, as related to him by Madge, is a glamorous memory and somehow it acts against the present reality of his more pedantic father — a good example of the past informing against the present. Gar, like Burke, has a strong commitment to the past. He is deeply attached to Ballybeg, the focus of the past. His former schoolmaster advises him: 'Be 100 per cent American' (p. 46). But although Gar realises the inadequacies of Ballybeg and calls it 'a bloody quagmire, a backwater, a dead-end!' (p. 81), his most nagging doubt is that by going away from Ballybeg, he will be leaving behind his roots, his sensitivities and his feelings. As such he joins the ranks of other vagrant characters in Irish drama: 'Since the beginning of this century, Irish drama has been heavily populated by people for whom vagrancy and exile have become inescapable conditions about which they can do nothing but talk, endlessly and eloquently and usually to themselves. The tramps of Yeats and Synge and Beckett, the stationless slum dwellers of O'Casey or Behan, bear a striking family resemblance to Friel's exiles.' (Seamus Deane in Introduction to *Selected Plays of Brian Friel.*)

Immediately following Public's recitation of the opening lines of Burke's *Reflections*, Private adopts the language of a cowboy: 'Let's git packin', boy, Let's git that li'l ole saddle bag opened and let's git packin'. The cowboy explored and opened up frontiers and in doing so he was involved in creating America's future. He took possession of a new landscape untouched by European tradition and culture. In some ways, the switching from one voice to another dramatises the conflict for Gar: the pull between the past and its emotional ties and the desire to create a new life for himself, a future identity.

The different cultural traditions which influence Gar are further highlighted when the 'cowboy' puts on 'a li'l ole music on the li'l ole phonograph'. The music is not a country-and-western favourite, but the First Movement of Mendelssohn's violin concerto. Mendelssohn represents the 'high art' music of European tradition. The mixture of images from past civilisations and those of the new world display the complex influences which affect Gar's mind in his search for a mature and stable identity. This subtle mixture of cultures is marvellously illustrated in Private's announcement of the beginning of Mendelssohn's concerto:

> The main item in tonight's concert is the First Movement of the Violin Concerto in E minor, Opus 64, by Jacob Ludwig Felix Mendelssohn. The orchestra is conducted by Gareth O'Donnell and the soloist is the Ballybeg half-back, Gareth O'Donnell. Music critics throughout the world claim that O'Donnell's simultaneous wielding of baton and bow is the greatest thing since Leather Ass died. Mendelssohn's Violin Concerto, First Movement.

Here Gareth O'Donnell, the conductor, represents the European tradition; Gareth O'Donnell, the Ballybeg half-back, represents the Gaelic tradition and his description of his performance as being 'the greatest thing since Leather Ass died', is representative of a Hollywood or American culture.

Gar's mother recalled

Gar examines the old suitcase that Madge has brought in.
He finds a sheet of faded newspaper inside the suitcase. This
leads him to thoughts about S.B.'s honeymoon and he recalls
what Madge has told him about his dead mother. (pp. 24-6)

COMMENTARY

THE old suitcase contains a sheet of faded newspaper dated 1st January 1937, the day Gar's parents were married. It would be a mistake to think that the date 1937 was chosen at random by Brian Friel. This date has a crucial significance and was selected deliberately. It immediately invokes an association with the setting up of the Irish Constitution of 1937. In many respects the play is a comment on the Ireland that emerged under that Constitution. The primacy of the family unit and the emphasis given to family life in that Constitution is put into ironic perspective by the portrayal of the marriages in the play.

Gar realises with a jolt that the suitcase hasn't been opened since his parents' honeymoon. His mind is flooded with images of his mother. His recollections of the facts concerning her provide us with new and important information which is vital to an understanding of the play. She died three days after his birth; she was a peasant girl; and by Madge's report, she was 'wild and young', the antithesis of Gar's father.

An important point to note here is that Gar's knowledge of his mother comes, not from his father, but through Madge: 'She was small, Madge says, and wild, and young, Madge says . . . she thought he was the grandest gentleman that ever lived, Madge says; and he — he couldn't take his eyes off her, Madge says . . .'. Gar's repetition of the phrase 'Madge says . . .' illustrates his child-like acceptance of her account. Gar's 'memory' of his mother is created from Madge's stories. The authenticity of these stories is accepted absolutely by Gar, and Madge is invoked as the validating authority. The Maire of Madge's stories is young, beautiful and free in spirit

— the epitome of youth. Even the name of her homeplace, Bailtefree, enhances this image. This may be an idealised version of Gar's mother, but it is in stark contrast to the ponderousness of S.B. Unwittingly, Madge's stories and her vivid descriptions help to alienate Gar from his father. In Gar's eyes his father somehow stands accused: 'And he must have known, old Screwballs, he must have known, Madge says, for many a night he must have heard her crying herself to sleep . . .'.

It would grieve Madge to know that she was in any way instrumental in causing a rift between Gar and S.B., especially when she clearly works to reconcile them. There are many instances in the play where she shows S.B. in a positive light: '. . . just because he doesn't say much doesn't mean that he hasn't feelings like the rest of us' (p. 20). When Gar asks her why his mother married S.B. rather than Master Boyle, she says: 'She married the better man by far' (p. 94). Her description of Gar's mother can be seen simply as a warm and loving recollection and it is Gar's interpretation of this description that causes him to feel that his father may be to blame for Maire's unhappiness.

S.B. and Maire's marriage was a short and not altogether happy one. Gar's mother became pregnant 'in that first year' and while friends of her own age were dressing up and going to dances, she was confined to home and to a much older husband. Her unhappiness was not concealed from S.B. From this claustrophobic environment, Private pictures her death as a welcome release: 'and maybe it was good of God to take her away three days after you were born'. Later in the play, Gar's father refers to the age difference between himself and his son and wonders if it was a contributing factor to the lack of communication between them. 'Maybe, Madge, maybe it's because I could have been his grandfather, eh?' (p. 107).

Apart from the vast difference in age between Gar's mother and S.B., there was also a contrast in their social upbringing. Gar's mother was a poor peasant girl ('she carried her shoes under her arm until she came to the edge of the village, Madge says, and then she put them on . . .'), while S.B. owned a shop. In rural Ireland, S.B. would have been considered a good marriage prospect. Maire's mother certainly approved of the marriage, as Aunt Lizzy reveals later: 'she thought that just because Maire got this guy with a big store we should all of got guys with big stores' (p. 59).

Gar's recollections are brought to an abrupt end and as Public struggles to erase the memories of the past, Private warns: 'Watch yourself, nut-head. If you let yourself slip that way, you might find that—'. Subconsciously, or coincidentally, Public supplies the words: '— right back where I started from'. These words from the popular song suggest that deep down Gar is aware that Philadelphia is not really the escape he longs for and that his loneliness and need to be affirmed will not be satisfied by his departure from Ballybeg. Philadelphia is one of Gar's fantasies. The rush of memories about his mother and the strength of his loyalty to Ballybeg create doubts in his mind about leaving.

The relief from memories of the past is short-lived and the music brings more recollections, this time about Kate Doogan.

 # Kate Doogan recalled

Public dances around the bedroom to the music of a ceilidhe band. Private reminds him that it was Kate's favourite tune. As Private taunts and cajoles him, Public produces a photograph of Kate from his wallet and there follows the memory of the night that Gar expressed his love for her and the humiliation of his visit to Senator Doogan's house. (pp. 26-35)

COMMENTARY

THIS is the first example in the play of Friel's use of the flashback technique. Up to now, the audience has been given glimpses of Gar's past life through his recollections and fantasies. But in this scene the audience actually sees the past enacted on stage. Gar's mind and his association of ideas is one of the organising principles in the play. His mind is selective and deals only with what is important at a given time. If the past is what most preoccupies him, it is the past that will be on stage before us.

The first part of this flashback takes us to a date ten months earlier and the details of Gar's courtship of Kate are revealed. Gar's emotional immaturity is clearly evident here. He shows a complete lack of awareness about the responsibilities of married life. He would like to be the father of fourteen children, but ignores all thoughts of financial security. Kate, who is more sensible and serious about such matters, protests that £3 15s is not enough to live on. Gar avoids the issue by kissing her hair and indulging in ridiculous speculation. Then, as Kate persists ('Please. This is serious'), Gar reveals the secret of the egg transaction whereby he gets 12s 6d to a £1, not every Tuesday and Thursday as Kate imagines at first, but every month. His ineptitude as a potential provider for a family is complete.

The second part of this flashback shows Gar in another light. He is confronted with the reality of asking Senator Doogan for Kate's hand in marriage. Fantasies and bravado are replaced by reticence and shyness. His legs tremble and he gropes desperately for the right words. In Senator Doogan's house 'instead of putting on a facade and indulging in fantasies, Gar does not act the clown, he *is* the clown in the original sense of the word — the clod, the lout, the awkward boor' (E. H. Winkler).

Senator Doogan, guessing at the reason for Gar's visit, quickly dispels any hope that Gar may have had of marrying Kate:

> Doogan: You've met Francis King, haven't you, Gareth?
> Public: Yes — Yes —
> Private: King of the bloody fairies!
> Doogan: We don't want to raise Kate's hopes unduly, but strictly between ourselves there's a good chance that he'll get the new dispensary job here.

Senator Doogan sees Kate as the wife of the local doctor, rather than as the wife of the grocer's son.

The social contrast between the O'Donnells and the Doogans is very evident here. The grocer's son is not good enough to marry the Senator's daughter. Doogan is more concerned with arranging a socially acceptable marriage than worrying about the happiness of his child: 'But if this post does fall into his lap, well, her mother and I . . . let's say we're living in hope.'

Faced with this knowledge, Gar is rejected, hurt and humiliated. His wounded feelings are reflected in Private's anguished remarks.

> O God, the aul bitch! Cripes, you look a right fool standing there — the father of fourteen children! Get out, you eejit you! Get out! Get out quick before the others come in and die laughing at you! And all the time she must have known — the aul bitch! And you promised to give her breakfast in bed every morning! And you told her about the egg money!

Even at the height of Private's agonising, Friel injects a humorous barb. For Gar, being made a fool of is bad enough, but the revelation of his closest secret — the tragically ludicrous secret of the egg-money — is almost too much for him to bear!

The light fades as the flashback comes to a close. Gar recalls details of Kate's wedding to Dr Francis King and admits to himself that the loss of Kate has left a deep scar on his soul. Public sings *Philadelphia, Here I Come!* in an effort to cloud out the painful memories. Private begins to console him: 'there's more fish in the sea', and he launches into a vindictive outburst about the private morals of the socially upright Senator: 'in his spare time he travels for maternity corsets; and . . . he's a double spy for the Knights and the Masons; and . . . he takes pornographic photographs of Mrs D. and sends them anonymously to reverend mothers'.

Out of this adolescent barrage against 'Mister Fair-play Lawyer Senator Doogan' comes an oblique reference to Gar's respect and affection for his father: 'And when you think of a bugger like that, you want to get down on your knees and thank God for aul Screwballs.' It will be recalled that S.B. married a poor, country girl. He was not concerned with the distinction of social class, a distinction which is uppermost in Senator Doogan's mind. Gar recognises that whatever faults S.B. O'Donnell may have, social snobbery is not one of them.

Role-playing and Fantasy

*Public carries on with his washing and dressing. Private
assumes the role of S.B. A dialogue follows about S.B.'s discomfort
when travelling. Then Gar's thoughts turn to America. Surveying
himself in the mirror, he imagines himself chatting to a gorgeous
American girl. (pp. 35-6)*

COMMENTARY

THERE are two parts to this sequence. Firstly, in a wonderfully comic
interlude, Gar imagines talking to his father about travel. The dialogue
is reminiscent of bawdy music-hall comedy. In sharp, punchy statements,
S.B. is presented as a man who suffers discomfort when he goes on a
journey.

> Private: Like the time I went to Lough Derg, away back in
> '35. Not a budge. The bare feet were nothing to the
> agonies I went through. I was bound up for two full
> weeks afterwards.
> Public: It taught you a lesson.
> Private: Didn't it just? Now I wouldn't even think about
> travelling.
> Public: Anchored by the ass.
> Private: Bound by the bowels.
> Public: Tethered by the toilet. Tragic.

Gar ironically infers that Ballybeg influences its inhabitants to such a
degree that leaving it causes upheaval and physical distress.

'Father' and 'son' talk quite naturally in this imagined dialogue. The
'conversation' displays none of the hesitancy of the everyday exchanges
between S.B. and Gar. This imagined dialogue deals with a delicate topic;
the language may be indecent, but it is the natural, free-flowing language of
intimates. Such dialogue is in total contrast to the actual speech of Gar and

S.B. where both 'embarrass' one another and communication is almost nonexistent.

In the second part of this sequence, Private adopts the role of a gorgeous American girl. The dialogue is delivered in an absurd Hollywood accent using words and phrases of American jargon: 'incinerator', 'elevator', 'slick operator', 'A malted milk at the corner drug-store', 'A movie at the downtown drive-in', 'Two hamburgers, two cokes, two slices of blueberry pie'. Gar is here rehearsing the sound of the American accent, but his images of America are of the same juvenile nature as his previous fantasies.

In a later scene we are to meet Gar's Aunt Lizzy on a visit from Philadelphia. Her perception of life in America consists of a list of items: 'We have this ground-floor apartment, see, and a car that's air-conditioned, and colour TV, and this big collection of all the Irish records you ever heard, and 15,000 bucks in Federal Bonds —'. For both aunt and nephew, the American dream is conceived in terms that are gross, vulgar and material.

The dialogue between Public and Private is accompanied by winks and nudges. The conversation is full of sexual innuendo: 'What'ya say, li'l chick, you and me — you know — I'll spell it out for ya if ya like. (*Winks, and clicks his tongue.*)' This sort of language and behaviour is typical of Gar and his contemporaries in Ballybeg. Later, we are to encounter the same innuendo and bawdy behaviour from Gar's friends, 'the boys', when they come to visit him. They all keep up a constant pretence of sexual bravado and banter, but this only hides the loneliness and frustration of their lives.

Madge and Gar

*Madge interrupts Gar's fantasy. She tells him about
the birth of her grandniece and her hope that the baby
will be named after her. We note Gar's reaction to this news.
(pp. 37-8)*

COMMENTARY

SOME aspects of the relationship between Gar and Madge are revealed in this short sequence. Madge occupies an important position in the O'Donnell household and is more than a housekeeper. She has cared for Gar since the death of his mother: 'I bathed you every Saturday night till you were a big lout of fourteen!' She is firm and confident in her dealings with him. She takes no nonsense or backchat from him and has a ready answer for each of his remarks. Gar's imminent departure is on her mind as shown by her comment, 'Dear, but you're in for a cooling when you go across!'

Madge and Gar are friends. She shyly confides to him the news of the birth of her grandniece: 'And they're going to call this one Madge —'.

However, the affection between them is rarely displayed overtly. Madge's acts of kindness and concern are discreet. She prepares his suitcase and irons his shirts. She slips money into his coat-pocket:

> That'll get him a cup of tea on the plane. I had put them two
> pounds by me to get my feet done on the fair day. But I can
> wait till next month. From what I hear, there's no big dances
> between now and then . . . (p. 108)

Madge makes up in some small way for S.B.'s failure to show affection. Gar's love for her is not translated into gestures or acts of kindness. It may be said that he takes her for granted. Yet he is possessive of her love and jealous when she bestows it on her own relatives.

Tea-time at O'Donnells'

S.B. enters and Private parodies the gestures and speech which always accompany the tea-time meal. Private longs for some word or gesture from S.B., some change in the banal ritual, especially on this, his last night at home. (pp. 38-43)

COMMENTARY

IT is interesting to note that in the scenes with his father, Public adopts a submissive, passive role. Although Gar is twenty-five years old, S.B. still treats him like a child. Gar replies in monosyllables to his father's questions about the shop, hoping that S.B. will make that 'one unpredictable remark', utter that one word of affection, which might prevent him going to Philadelphia. When this remark is not forthcoming, Public vents his frustration by roaring for the bread. His father upbraids him for shouting and Public stammers a halting apology: 'I'll — I'll get it myself — it doesn't matter . . .' When S.B. produces Gar's wages, Public sullenly says that he has earned the money and that he wasn't going to count it. He offers his father another cup of tea but is greeted once again by the predictable response: 'Sure you know I never take a second cup'. The lack of communication is complete.

Public's verbal contribution in this scene amounts to nine utterances. Of these the first two are only grunted responses of 'Aye, Aye'. The others are as follows: '(roars) Madge! Madge!'; 'The-the-the bread's done. We need more bread.'; 'Can we have more bread, Madge . . . please . . .'; 'I'll — I'll get it myself — it doesn't matter . . .'; 'I earned it.'; 'I didn't say I was going to count it, did I?'; and 'More tea?' It is clear that Public is every bit as recalcitrant in open speech as his father. Madge's later prophecy that S.B. and Gar are 'as like as two peas' is seen to be very close to the truth. Through Private's portrayal of Gar's inner self, with its variety of fantasy, imagination, memory and speculation, the audience can see the hidden side of Gar's personality. Without this revelation Gar's utterances would appear as banal and pedantic as his father's.

Later in the play we are to get a glimpse of S.B.'s inner thoughts when he divulges to Madge his memory of taking Gar to school:

> and, d'you mind, you tried to coax him to go to school, and not a move you could get out of him, and him as manly looking, and this wee sailor suit as smart looking on him, and — and — and at the heel of the hunt I had to go with him myself, the two of us, hand in hand, as happy as larks . . . (p. 107)

As Friel's main concern is with the unravelling of Gar's character, he preserves the disclosure of S.B.'s private memories until the last episode of the play. Up to then, the audience may have doubted that S.B. was capable of displaying any sensitivity or emotion. He has barricaded himself inside an attitude of formality and detachment. When talking to Gar, his speech is perfunctory and unexpressive. He has such a limited repertoire of responses that the audience begins to wonder whether he has an interior life at all. Private verbalises these uncertainties about S. B.'s apparent lack of emotion when he asks later: 'God — maybe — Screwballs — behind those dead eyes and that flat face are there memories of precious moments in the past?' (p. 89). But the tragedy of the play is that although Gar and S.B. have precious memories, they cannot communicate them to each other.

Friel dealt with this theme of unshared memories in his earlier short story, *Among the Ruins*. Joe, the father in the story, takes his wife and children back to the place where he was born. But he realises that the visit was a mistake: 'He should never have gone back, he knew; at least, he should have never have gone back with Margo and the children. Because the past is a mirage — a soft illusion into which one steps in order to escape the present!'

The visit robbed him of his precious memories and his illusions about the past, 'and in their place now there was nothing — nothing at all but the truth'. However, for Joe there is some redemption and at the end of the story he realises that the past was more than a mirage:

> The past did have meaning. It was neither reality nor dreams, neither today's patchy oaks nor the great woods of his boyhood. It was simply continuance, life repeating itself and surviving.

No such illumination affects S.B. and Gar at the end of this play. In fact the agonising and continuing lack of communication between the two is the central tragedy of *Philadelphia*.

While Public sits almost speechless, Private continues his satirical mimicry. His parody of S.B. as a mannequin in a fashion parade — 'The pert little apron is detachable —' is one of the comic highlights of the play. But the humorous tone of this parody gives way to a more bitter satire by Private. As the scene goes on, 'all traces of humour fade from Private's voice. He becomes more and more intense and it is with an effort that he keeps his voice under control'. As S.B. doles out his ritual banalities, Private longs for 'one unpredictable remark', some hint or acknowledgement that S.B. would wish him to stay, but the sad fact is that in each other's company, father and son 'embarrass one another'.

In an emotive sequence, Private almost loses control of himself as he makes a direct appeal to his father for some communication. The tragic irony is that the appeal is made by Private whose voice is only an echo in Gar's mind. The audience can hear the 'unspoken' thoughts of Gar: S.B. is not thus privileged. Private's suggestions for that 'one unpredictable remark' range from the poetic to the vulgar:

> So now, Screwballs, say . . . (thinks) . . . 'Once upon a time a rainbow ended in our garden' . . . say 'I like to walk across the White Strand when there's a misty rain falling' . . . say, 'Gar, son —' say, 'Gar, you bugger you, why don't you stick it out here with me for it's not such a bad aul bugger of a place.' Go on. Say it! Say it! Say it!

But S.B.'s remarks are simply a repetition of his earlier comment about the number of rats which were about the place during the year. Gar's unspoken hopes for a change in the pattern are not realised. Private reverts back to his former brittle and bright self and accepts that 'you can't teach new tricks to two old dogs like us'. He proceeds with his mimicry, this time with an hilarious, if somewhat tragic, parody of a son talking to his father about the facts of life. He is interrupted eventually by the arrival of Master Boyle.

Master Boyle's Visit

Master Boyle, shabbily dressed, enters from the scullery and fidgets
around the kitchen. S.B. leaves very quickly and is 'barely
courteous to him'. Boyle tells Gar about his rows with the Canon,
and reminisces about the Gallagher girls. He produces a book of
his own poetry, gives it to Gar and asks for a loan of 10s. Gar gives
him a pound and Boyle embraces him. Then the Master rushes out,
bumping into Madge on his way. Public, who is emotionally upset
by his former teacher's show of affection, runs to his bedroom. He
stands inside the bedroom door with his hands to his face recalling
his mother, Kate Doogan and the Master's words. Private speaks
urgently and tries to cloud out the images of the past with
fantasised images of life in America. Both Public and Private end
the episode by singing Philadelphia, Here I Come! (pp. 43-8)

COMMENTARY

S.B.'s hasty departure from the kitchen, when Master Boyle comes in, could be interpreted in a number of ways. The stage direction indicates that S.B. is 'barely courteous to him', yet he addresses Boyle formally with his full title 'Master', and offers him his seat. The formal tone is perhaps S.B.'s way of distancing himself from Boyle — of denying Boyle any claim of friendship or intimacy in the O'Donnell household. S.B. is respectful and displays none of the sarcasm or bitterness of Private's early remarks ('On his way to the pub! God, but he's a sorry wreck too, arrogant and pathetic'), or of Madge's at the end of the scene ('Lord, the speed of him! His tongue out for a drink!').

Master Boyle is the antithesis of the responsible, respectable citizen of Ballybeg. He is an alcoholic, dresses shabbily and has an air of defiance which is expressed in his continuous rows with the Canon. S.B.'s hasty departure could be attributed to the fact that he is friendly with Canon Mick O'Byrne: they play draughts together every night in the O'Donnell house. The Canon and Master Boyle are in conflict and disputes between them are commonplace. It may be inferred that Gar is sympathetic towards Master Boyle in this conflict, whereas S.B. sides with the Canon.

S.B. has another reason for being 'barely courteous' towards the Master. They were rivals in love. In an exchange between Gar and Madge later in the play (pp. 94-95), we discover that Boyle had courted Gar's mother before she married S.B. It is also suggested that her rejection of him may have led to Boyle's drinking problem.

> Public: But is that what started Boyle drinking?
> Madge: If it was, more fool he . . .

Master Boyle's visit to the O'Donnell house is motivated by a genuine interest and concern about Gar's departure but it is also tainted by a certain amount of pettiness. Three traits of Boyle's character emerge during this visit. Firstly, Boyle is exposed as an envious man. He has his fantasies, just like Gar, but his fantasies are more pathetic, coming as they do from a man in his sixties. He still dreams of escaping to America: his supposed offer of a big post as head of a university in Boston is absolute escapism and as childish as any of Gar's fantasies. This wishful thinking reflects his frustration with Ballybeg and he envies Gar his opportunity of escaping. Gar sees through the pathetic nature of Boyle's fantasies, even though he does not draw a parallel between the hopelessness of the Master's aspirations and his own equally idealistic dreams.

Secondly, Boyle shows himself to be self-centered. He considers himself more intellectually dominant than Gar and wastes no opportunity to 'get the dig in'. He says to Gar: 'You're young and strong and of average intelligence.' Later, when he gives Gar a book of his own poems, he says 'Some of them are a bit mawkish but you'll not notice any distinction.' Boyle displays another aspect of his self-centredness by asking Gar to send him the addresses of newspapers or magazines 'that might be interested in an occasional poem'.

Finally, Boyle shows a pathetic lack of dignity. Throughout his conversation with Gar, he keeps looking at the clock. Constant fidgetting, eyes roaming around the room but seeing nothing, sitting for a moment then rising again — all his gestures betray the symptoms of alcoholism. His lack of dignity and respect is typified by borrowing a pound from his former pupil in full knowledge that he will not be able to repay the debt.

Gar sees Boyle as being a 'sorry wreck, arrogant and pathetic', but yet he holds a certain affection for him. The expression of this affection comes as Boyle recalls the Gallagher girls and Private says: 'You might have been my father'. Coming as it does after the debacle of the tea-time scene, Boyle displays more paternal affection towards Gar in his short visit than S.B. does in the whole play. In the words of one observer, he is the 'surrogate father who has fed Gareth's blind yearnings as surely as his true father has starved his spirit', *(Time* Review). It is the first time in the play that anybody has voluntarily expressed a sense of loss at Gar's departure. Coming as it does from a 'drunken aul school-master — a conceited, arrogant wash-out!', we can imagine the affect a show of emotion from S.B. might have had on Gar.

The sequence in which Boyle embraces Gar is the emotional highlight of Episode 1, yet Friel uses simple, rather than ornate or poetic, language to convey intensity of feeling:

> Boyle: Good luck, Gareth.
> Public: Thanks, Master.
> Boyle: Forget Ballybeg and Ireland.
> Public: It's easier said.
> Boyle: Perhaps you'll write me.
> Public: I will indeed.
> Boyle: Yes, the first year. Maybe the second. I'll — I'll miss you, Gar.
> Private: For God's sake get a grip on yourself.
> Public: Thanks for the book and for — *(Boyle embraces Public briefly.)*
> Private: Stop it! Stop it! Stop it!

It will be remembered that Madge had to be coerced into admitting that she would miss Gar, but here Master Boyle expresses his emotions freely. Gar reacts to the embrace with confused numbness, an attitude he again displays when he is embraced by Aunt Lizzy later in the play. She comments that the O'Donnells are 'kinda cold'. Gar and S.B. are incapable of showing their true affections and both recoil from outward displays of affection although yearning for deep communication.

Gar is emotionally shattered after Master Boyle's embrace. Private immediately resorts to abuse, song and fantasy, while Public struggles with memories of his mother and of Kate Doogan. He almost succumbs to the pull of memories of his loved ones, and as Private reminds him about going to America he says: 'I don't — I can't'. But finally the promptings of Private take effect and both end the episode singing *Philadelphia, Here I Come!* Their limp rendering of the theme-song provides a sharp contrast to the joy and excitement of the opening scene.

EPISODE 2

Keeping up the spirits

Episode 2 opens with Public lying on the bed singing a slow Irish air, She Moved through the Fair. Private springs to his feet and rouses Public with lively banter, jokes, fantasy and song. The sound of Madge in the kitchen brings Gar back to reality. (pp. 51-4)

COMMENTARY

EPISODE 2 begins on a sombre note. The gusto and fervour of the song *Philadelphia, Here I Come!* is replaced by the slow Irish air *She Moved through the Fair*. Gar is still emotionally shattered after Master Boyle's display of affection. The pendulum of his thoughts has swung away from the carefree abandonment of his future in Philadelphia, towards his Irish heritage and the emotional ties of Ballybeg.

Private tries to redress the balance and prevent Public from getting swallowed up in sentimentality. Public is less than enthusiastic about getting involved in banter, jokes, fantasy and song; he is almost a reluctant straightman in a vaudeville comedy act. But Private's persistence pays off and Public finally enters the spirit of the entertainment which involves a fantasy in which 'Senator Gareth O'Donnell, Chairman of the Foreign Aid Committee', investigates Senator Doogan and a Chinese spy named Screwballs. The sound of Madge in the kitchen puts a sudden stop to the hilarity and Private, exhausted from his efforts, drops wearily into an armchair and says: 'You know what you're doing, don't you, laddybuck? Collecting memories and images and impressions that are going to make you bloody miserable; and in a way that's what you want, isn't it?' (p. 54).

The returned emigrants

*Gar checks his immigration documents and produces a letter written
to him by his Aunt Lizzy. In the second flashback of the play, Con
Sweeney, Aunt Lizzy and Ben Burton appear on stage. It is the day
of Kate Doogan's wedding to Dr Francis King. There follows a
conversation recalling details of Con and Lizzy's emigration to
Philadelphia, interspersed with memories of Maire and S.B.'s
wedding day. The sequence ends with Gar deciding to go to
Philadelphia and Lizzy throwing her arms around him. (pp. 54-66)*

COMMENTARY

LIZZY Gallagher, Gar's boozy, garrulous aunt, dominates this scene. Gar,
who has never seen his mother, cannot take his eyes off her, searching,
perhaps, for an image of his mother. Lizzy tells us that Maire and herself
were 'so alike in every way'. This may account for Gar's fixation, and may
also explain why S.B. fails to meet her during her stay in Ballybeg. She
comments on his absence: 'Where the hell is he anyhow? Why will S.B.
O'Donnell, my brother-in-law, not meet me?' (p. 59).

S.B. is attending the wedding of Kate Doogan and there is a certain
irony in the fact that Gar, who would have liked to be the bridegroom, does
not attend. Friel uses the occasion of Aunt Lizzy's visit to highlight the three
marriages depicted in the play, marriages which share and repeat a pattern
of disappointment and failure.

Marriage in its ideal state is a union of love which fulfils the
individual and gives a sense of completion to life. It has a sacramental
reality and the importance of family love is enshrined in the Irish
Constitution. But the social reality is often different. Marriage as an
institution can sometimes bring a sense of disappointment and failure. Kate
Doogan marries Dr Francis King, not because she loves him, but because
her parents are anxious that she marry into the proper social class. King is
a graduate, a doctor and hence, in her parents' eyes, a suitable husband.

Maire's marriage to S.B. may not have been a love match either. Madge reveals, later in the play, that Gar's mother was courted by Master Boyle: 'she went with a dozen — that was the kind of her — she couldn't help herself' (p. 95). She was a young, spirited, attractive girl, yet she married S.B., a dull, pedantic man, twenty-one years her senior. Lizzy's description of Maire's wedding day makes us wonder whether Maire was happy or sad on that occasion: '— and up at the altar rails there's Maire all by herself and her shoulders are sorta working — you know — and you couldn't tell whether she was crying or giggling — she was a helluva one for giggling — but maybe she was crying that morning — I don't know —' (p. 57). Maire's mother certainly approved of the marriage: S.B. owned a grocery and hardware shop and as such he was seen as a suitable marriage partner.

In Lizzy's case, her feelings for her husband are ambiguous: most of her remarks about him are disparaging — she calls him 'bonzo' and sarcastically refers to him as 'Rudolph Valentino', the famous screen lover of the silent movie era. She reserves her embraces and kisses for Ben Burton and proclaims his generosity and friendship: 'He gives us this apartment. He gives us dough. He gives us three meals a day — until bonzo *(Con)* finally gets himself this job. Looks after us like we were his own skin and bone'. Con, her quiet, patient husband is castigated by Lizzy, yet he stands by her and supports her. In an interview with Peter Lennon of the *Guardian* (October 8th, 1964) Friel commented on the relationship between Con, Lizzy and Ben: 'I think you find that a lot in Irish marriages, there is another man floating like a satellite around the couple. A person in whom the wife confides, probably. There is nothing sinister in this and certainly nothing sexual . . .'.

The marriages of the play fail to provide a sense of fulfilment or completion in the lives of the participants. The substance of life is almost destroyed by these marriages. Paradoxically, the birth of a child, which should affirm life, has robbed Maire of her own life, while Con and Lizzy desperately long for a child to affirm their love, but are denied it by a cruel twist of fate.

Lizzy uses Ben Burton as a way of expressing her disappointment with Con and with the failure of their marriage to produce a child. Implicitly and explicitly she is disparaging of her husband. However, when she breaks down on stage ('And it's all so Gawd-awful because we have no one to share it with us . . .'), it is Con, her husband, who comforts her *('(softly)* It's okay, honey, okay . . .'). Ben withdraws and goes to collect the car round the front. Thus we see that Lizzy's relationship with Ben is not a threat to her marriage. The longing for a child is what unites Con and Lizzy. Yet, it separates them, causing her to vent her frustration and disappointment on her husband. Con's knowledge of her frustration and his own sense of disappointment makes him sympathetic and patient. He accepts her public humiliation of him, knowing the anguish from which the remarks have sprung.

Ben Burton represents all that America has to offer the Irish immigrants. He is generous and has given an unconditional welcome to the Sweeneys. There are no strings attached to his generosity — he is not interested in selfgain. In a material sense, America is the land of opportunity and plenty. Lizzy shows a constant preoccupation with money and material possessions. She presents an air of confidence and superiority. She has adopted the self-assurance of American society, a belief that no matter how poor or humble your background, you can succeed. The barriers of social class, illustrated by Gar's encounter with Senator Doogan, prevail in Ballybeg, but will not hinder one's progress in the 'new world'. Lizzy's dazzling performance testifies to the American dream, but beneath the facade, the hollowness of material wealth and possessions is revealed.

Lizzy has all the ambiguous characteristics of the returned exile. She is American, yet she is possessive of her Irish identity and resentful of an American claiming a superior knowledge of Ireland: 'Don't you start telling me nothing about my own country, Ben. You got your own problems to look after. Just you leave me to manage this place, okay?' (p. 60). Although Lizzy claims to be a 'good Irish-American Catholic', she is at home in neither country. Ben, the American, exudes a calm assurance and confidence; Lizzy, the exile, unsure of her Irish or American identity, projects an uncertain, hence artificial, personality.

Lizzy feels a sense of superiority over those who remain behind in Ballybeg. She constantly refers to her possessions and wealth. Her exaggerated self-confidence and brashness is revealed in her sarcastic comment to Madge: 'Doing big deals out there, honey, huh?' (p. 60). Friel's stage direction reveals Madge's attitude to the returned exiles: 'she refuses to look at the visitors. Her face is tight with disapproval. Her accent is very precise.' Perhaps this is a natural reaction of a quiet person towards someone who is loud, garrulous and brash: 'Never had much time for blatherin' women . . .' (p. 102). Madge had already been critical of Gar's 'eejiting about' and, later, she castigates Gar's friends for being over-robust and loud when they come to visit him. But her main reason for ignoring

Lizzy and disapproving of her behaviour can be seen in a different light. Madge and Lizzy are rivals for Gar's affection. Madge's maternal relationship with Gar is threatened by Lizzy. In a contest for Gar, Madge knows that she cannot win — she has nothing to offer him in material terms except the two pound notes which she puts into his coat pocket towards the end of the play. Lizzy, on the other hand has all the seductive trappings of wealth with which to lure Gar away from Madge's affections.

Madge adopts an air of dignity as a way of showing her disapproval of Lizzy's lack of restraint. She puts on a formal and dignified air ('Thank you, Gareth.'). This contrasts with the informality of Lizzy's 'Honey'. Lizzy lacks Madge's dignity. In Ballybeg, title and formality are very important. S.B. always calls the Canon by his title and even the drunken schoolteacher is referred to as 'Master'. This formality creates a rigidity in Madge's and S.B.'s relationships with other people. They have difficulty in communicating their real feelings, while Lizzy touches and embraces people and blurts out all her anguish. Both sides could learn something from each other: Lizzy, some dignity, and the people of Ballybeg, a degree of informality and warmth.

This scene highlights the dramatic moment when Gar committed himself to emigrating to Philadelphia. But there are hints of his deep uncertainty about this commitment. He made a promise to Lizzy, a promise that was easily extracted, but as the play goes on, he has less and less desire to fulfil it. We hear Gar's opinion of Aunt Lizzy. He has reservations about her because of her vulgarity, her bad grammar, and her smothering, overwhelming longing for a child of her own: 'She'll tuck you into your air-conditioned cot every night . . . And croon, "Sleep well, my li'l honey child" ' (p. 65).

Initially, Gar was lukewarm about the prospects of emigration to Philadelphia:

> Con: You'll think about what we were discussing?
>
> Public: I will, Uncle Con.
>
> Con: The job's as good as you'll get and we'd be proud to have you.
>
> Lizzy: Don't force him.
>
> Con: I'm not forcing him. I'm only telling him.
>
> Lizzy: Well now, you've told him — a dozen times. So now desist, will you?
>
> *(Con spreads his hands.)*
>
> Public: I will think about it. Really.

Although Lizzy has just reprimanded Con for trying to force Gar to make up his mind, she now launches into an attack at her nephew's lack of decisiveness: 'Sure! Sure! Typical Irish! He will think about it! And while he's thinking about it the store falls in about his head!' But Lizzy's sarcasm does not provoke Gar into making a decision. The two major factors which influence him are firstly, the loss of his sweetheart Kate to Dr Francis King ('She got you soft on account of the day it was, didn't she?), and secondly, Gar's rejection of Lizzy's remark that the O'Donnells were 'kinda cold'. Gar, motherless Gar, cannot bear to be associated with the cold, unemotional traits of his father. His need for affection and love makes him identify with his mother's family. His initial response to the question of emigration could almost have come from S.B. ('I will think about it. Really'), but at the prospect of being termed cold and unaffectionate, he almost foists himself upon his Aunt Lizzy. The coldness of his father gives him a compelling reason to associate with the 'laughing, crying, impetuous' Gallaghers.

Friel captures the sense of Gar's identity crisis — O'Donnell or Gallagher — in a moving and highly emotional sequence in which Gar accepts and rejects Lizzy's affection. With Private saying 'Don't man, don't', Public makes his commitment.

> Public: *(impetuously)* I want to go to America — if you'll
>   have me . . .
> Lizzy: If we'll have him, he says; he says if we'll have him!
>   That's why I'm here! That's why I'm half-shot up!
>   . . . Oh Gar, my son —
> Private: Not yet! Don't touch me yet!
>   *(Lizzy throws her arms around him and cries*
>   *happily.)*
> Lizzy: My son, Gar, Gar, Gar . . .
> Private: *(softly, with happy anguish)* God . . . my God . . . Oh
>   my God . . .

Gar decides to reject the O'Donnell coldness for the warmth and affection of the Gallagher nature. He tries to assert the 'difference' between himself and his father. The irony of this assertion is that Gar Public displays many of the characteristics of his father. Madge's comment towards the end of the play highlights this fact: Gar and S.B. are 'as like as two peas. And when he's *(Gar)* the age the boss is now, he'll turn out just the same.'

The words that hurt the most

*Gar, recoiling from the emotion of the previous scene with
Aunt Lizzy and tormented by the taunting of Private, is curt
and impatient with Madge. She in turn vents her frustration at
S.B. who is totally puzzled by her uncharacteristic outburst.
S.B., who has been 'reading' his newspaper upside down, looks
across at Gar's bedroom, sighs, rises and exits to the shop.*
(pp. 66-7)

COMMENTARY

THE tension between the main characters becomes very evident at this
point. Gar's remarks to Madge are uncharacteristically curt and
abusive. 'If you would only learn to leave things where you find them you
wouldn't be such a bad aul nuisance'; 'And how I spend my nights is a
matter entirely for myself'; 'Just you mind your business and I'll mind
mine'. The irony of the latter statement is revealed later when Gar is
confronted with the knowledge that Madge invited 'the boys' to visit the
O'Donnell house. Madge doubts that they would have come without this
invitation.

The exchanges between Madge and Gar in this sequence can be
compared to those between Gar and his father. Although Madge and Gar
are talking to each other, their actual words do not communicate their real
feelings. When Gar tells Madge that he wants a call at half-six, she replies:
'The clock'll be set. If you hear it well and good.' Madge is implying that it is
a matter of total indifference to her whether Gar gets called or not, whereas
the reality is very different.

The mock taunting between them clearly upsets Madge very much.
She fusses about the kitchen and then vents her frustration at S.B. in a
tearful outburst. S.B., who was not present during the exchanges between
Gar and Madge, is totally bewildered by her outburst. Madge is obviously
overcome by the impending departure of Gar for Philadelphia. She realises

that if S.B. were to say one word of encouragement, if he were to give one hint that he wanted his son to stay, he might prevent Gar's departure. Her hopes had been expressed earlier in the play: 'just because he doesn't say much doesn't mean that he hasn't feelings like the rest of us'. Now as she watches him read the newspaper, her earlier optimism that he'll have something to say has faded and she knows that S.B. will be a silent observer of a leavetaking he might have prevented. Her frustration is directed at his total lack of concern or appreciation for herself. If he had any respect for her, he would keep his false teeth in while there's 'a lady' in his presence! As the tears begin to fall; she tries to blot out the hurt and frustration by thinking about her household chores — the washing, sweeping and cleaning . . . 'I'm telling you, I'll be that busy for the next couple of weeks that I won't have time to lift my head!'

S. B. betrays the fact that he too is upset about Gar's impending departure. The newspaper he was 'reading' is upside-down. He looks across at Gar's bedroom and sighs. Then, slowly, he goes out to the shop. Screwballs, the Chinese spy of Gar's earlier fantasy who seldom speaks and is 'a man of few words', expresses his feelings in gestures. As a reviewer in *Time* magazine observed: 'Gareth's father puts on his glasses to see the paper, never his son. Yet there is a kind of love between the two, all the more painful for being inarticulate. The words that hurt the most on this final evening together are the words that are not said.'

The visit of 'the boys'

The silence is shattered by the arrival of 'the boys'. Gar is initially flattered by their visit, but gradually his good humour deserts him. He sets himself aside from the others and when he discovers that Madge invited 'the boys' to see him off, he is totally disillusioned and launches into a vehement attack on his friends. The mood of this attack changes and he takes a nostalgic look back on his time spent with his friends in Ballybeg. He realises that his youthful 'adventures' in Ballybeg are a thing of the past.
(pp. 68-79)

COMMENTARY

THE boisterous arrival of 'the boys' lightens the tension of the previous hours. It is worth noting the stage direction here. 'The boys' give 'the impression that they are busy, purposeful, randy gents about to embark on some exciting adventure. But their bluster is not altogether convincing. There is something false about it. Tranquility is their enemy: they fight it valiantly.'

Gar is obviously delighted that 'the boys' have come to visit him. He has yet to discover that they have come on Madge's invitation and their visit was not inspired by any great loyalty to him. When Madge enters, she sarcastically comments on their noisy, raucous behaviour: 'Just thought I heard somebody whispering. So youse finally made it'. Joe replies: 'True to our word, Madge, that's us!' Gar misses the significance of this exchange and happily tells Madge that his friends were on their way to visit him when he ran into them.

'The boys' embody much of the fantasy and role-playing already displayed by Private. They take refuge in loud, bawdy talk about their exploits, but these are grossly exaggerated and distorted. We realise that pretence plays an important part in the lives of Gar and his contemporaries in Ballybeg. 'All of them put on a constant show of sexual and physical prowess and keep up a continuous flow of bantering talk in order to avoid admitting how lonely, boring, and sexually frustrated their ordinary lives are' (Winkler, p. 143).

The term 'boys' is a misnomer. We know that Gar is twenty-five years old and his friends are around the same age. Madge's sarcastic remarks, 'Boys! How are you!' (p. 69) and 'How many of them are getting the pension now?' (p. 66), highlight this fact and makes their childish, adolescent posturing all the more tragic.

Friel's detailed stage direction gives us an insight into the relationships between 'the boys': 'Ned is the leader of the group. Tom is his feed-man, subserviently watching for every cue. Joe, the youngest of the trio, and not yet fully committed to the boys' way of life, is torn between fealty to Ned and Tom and a spontaneous and simple loneliness over Gar's departure. Nothing would suit him better than a grand loud send-off party. But he cannot manage this, and his loyalty is divided. He is patently gauche, innocent, obvious.'

Gar tries several times to raise the issue of his impending departure, but each time Ned cuts across these remarks and quickly changes the subject:

> Public: *(raising glass)* Well, boys, when you're lining out on the pitch, you can think of me, because I'll be thinking of you.
>
> Joe: *(earnestly)* Lucky bloody man, Gar. God, I wish I was in your —
>
> Ned: *(quickly)* By the way, lads, who's the blondie thing I seen at the last Mass on Sunday? (p. 69)

'If the "boys" were to talk about Gar's impending departure, his hopes and his prospects, they would have to admit to the realities of their own lives, their constant disappointments and frustrations, their own lack of prospects. For this reason they choose to ignore the fact that he is leaving' (Winkler, p. 143).

Ned's recollection of being out with Annie McFadden is distorted like many of the other memories in the play. S.B.'s memory of the sailor-suit, Gar's memory of the fishing-trip and Aunt Lizzy's faulty recollections of dates and events, may be attributed to their desire to remember the good times only. Their memories are selective, ignoring bad experiences and remembering happy times. Ned's faulty memory, however, is a deliberate distortion of the facts in order to enhance his self-image as a cavalier, sexual conqueror: 'I had her for the fortnight she was home last year and she damned near killed me'. Even a physical characteristic like a squint can be 'cured' in Ned's version of the past. When Joe points out that Annie McFadden had a squint, Ned strenuously denies this. Joe backs down and says, 'And maybe she got the squint straightened out since I saw her last'. Here Friel inserts comic relief into a potentially aggressive situation.

The silence that ensues allows Private to survey the group. 'The boys . . . They weren't always like this, were they? There was a hell of a lot of crack, wasn't there? There was a hell of a lot of laughing, wasn't there?' These rhetorical questions show that Gar is doubting his own recollections of his time with 'the boys'. He is studiously objective now, he doesn't like what he sees and what he was once part of. Tom and Ned continue the contrived references to sexual conquest, but the audience, Joe, and Gar know that there is little substance or credibility attached to anything they say. When Private tells the real story of the night with Gladys and Susan, we see just how much Ned and Tom have exaggerated their version of events. Ned is not only a braggart, but a coward as well: 'But when Ned started towards Jimmy — five foot nothing, remember? — wee Jimmy squared up and defied not only the brave Ned but the whole lot of us. So we straggled back home, one behind the other, and left the girls dangling their feet in the water. And that was that night' (p. 73).

The visit of 'the boys' is another example of lack of communication in the play. Ostensibly, 'the boys' have come to the O'Donnell house to wish Gar farewell, but instead they avoid conversation about his departure and engage in monologues about themselves and their exploits. Their reluctance to recognise, or speak about, Gar's impending exile is like the reaction of S.B., Madge, Canon O'Byrne, and, even Master Boyle. Gar is isolated from the other inhabitants of Ballybeg. Their failure to speak about his exile, his reasons for going, his plans for the future, is a subtle pressure which Gar must overcome. 'Before he can enter the jet, he must wrench himself from the womb of place. To be reborn, he must be unborn. He must blot out the streets and scents of Ballybeg. He must stop his ears against the voices of friends and their loutish camaraderie. He must stiffen in the embrace of the drunken schoolmaster, a surrogate father who has fed Gareth's blind yearnings as surely as his true father has starved his spirit. And he must face the vision of what he may become, in the person of a blowsy ginned-up Irish-American aunt who is making his exodus to America possible.' (*Time* review, 1966).

Ned's only concession to the fact that Gar is leaving is expressed in his awkward parting-gift. He takes off his broad leather belt with the huge brass buckle and, in confusion, flings it across the room to Gar. Ned is torn between a genuine expression of friendship towards Gar and his need to maintain appearances: he cannot appear soft or sentimental in front of his friends. His henchman, Tom, fails to detect the change of mood in Ned. Ned turns on him, giving him more than a playful punch while saying savagely: 'Christ, if there's one get I hate, it's you!' Tom, faithful to the last, doesn't realise when the fooling has to stop. He is a gormless dupe and cannot understand why he has been attacked. He follows Ned like a faithful dog who trails his master.

Joe is left alone with Gar: his loyalties are confused. He knows that the exploits of Ned and Tom are all a pretence and he'd still like to give Gar a rousing send-off. But Gar realises that in Ballybeg, fantasy is the only consolation for Joe and his friends. He encourages Joe to . . . 'Get to hell and run after them' . . . 'For God's sake, man, those English women will be swept off their feet!' . . . 'I'm telling you, you're missing the chance of a lifetime.' With a little encouragement from Gar, Joe begins to believe in the fantasy. Life in Ballybeg is more bearable if it is brightened by make-believe. Gar realises this and does not wish to deprive Joe of his fabricated world: otherwise he would be condemning Joe to the loneliness and boredom of the real world.

Before Joe leaves, he reveals that Madge had invited them to the house for a cup of tea. Whatever consolation Gar had gained from the visit of 'the boys' is totally shattered: 'She *asked* you?' he says incredulously. Earlier, he had glowingly told Madge that his friends 'were on their way here when I ran into them'. Now he knows that Madge was instrumental in their coming to see him. Gar drops all sense of loyalty towards his friends and castigates them: 'They're louts, ignorant bloody louts, and you've always known it!' But the tone of his invective changes and he realises 'but for Aunt Lizzy and the grace of God' he'd be with his friends tonight. With an air of wistful nostalgia, he knows that he will never again join 'the boys' in their fantastic exploits. He answers the questions which he had asked himself at the beginning of this scene: 'there *was* fun and there *was* laughing — foolish, silly fun and foolish, silly laughing'. Gar will distil the memory of all its coarseness and what remains will be 'precious, precious gold'.

Kate's visit

*Kate enters and an awkward conversation ensues between
herself and Gar. Gar's tone gets louder and more aggressive as
the dialogue goes on. Private attempts to calm Public but when
Kate mentions his father, Gar delivers a scathing speech against
Ballybeg and its inhabitants. Kate leaves and Public buries his
face in his hands. He recalls the night of his 'proposal' to Kate,
and the memory of this experience is interspersed with other
recollections from Episode 1: 'gut and salt them fish'; 'and
they're going to call this one Madge'; 'a little something to
remind you of your old teacher'. The final whispered shout, a
cry of anguish for his father to say something, brings Episode 2
to a close. (pp. 79-83)*

COMMENTARY

THE arrival of Kate causes confusion and reticence in Gar. He is not sure
how to react. Private urges him to 'Talk! Talk!' and at first he speaks in
a casual, slightly off-hand, manner. In outlining his plans for the future, Gar
reveals that he is still smarting from the rebuke and derision he felt after
his meeting with Senator Doogan. Doogan and the father of Dr Francis King
went to university together: the former did law, the latter, medicine. Gar
tells Kate that he will probably go to night-school in Philadelphia and 'do
law or medicine or something'. This is an effort to meet the standard of the
Doogans. Private castigates him: 'Like hell! First Arts stumped you!'
Although these plans must sound hollow in Kate's ears, she does not deprive
him of his illusions: 'You'll do well, Gar; make a lot of money, and come back
here in twenty years' time, and buy the whole village.'

It is worth noting that in this scene Private is the one who tries to
calm Public. Up to now, Public has been the more restrained, while Private
in long, eloquent speeches has given full vent to his frustrations. But when
Gar is alone with Kate he is not restricted in his speech. As Winkler points

out: 'Gar speaks and acts "aggressively" and "recklessly", and his hard-boiled posturing prevents any meaningful contact with his former sweetheart. Gar is trying to protect himself and hide his wounded feelings, as Private's anguished remarks show, and he does this in the only way he knows how, by putting on a show. Here, however, all humour has vanished. Because he has been so deeply hurt by Kate's marriage to another, Gar can no longer joke or mimic in her presence. But he continues to play, to overact his role, hiding behind an exaggerated aggressiveness and a pretended nonchalance. The function of the role-playing has remained the same: self-protection and evasion of the unpleasant; only the form has changed.'

At the mention of his father, Gar becomes more and more aggressive. Kate's sensitive remark 'Your father'll miss you', produces an outburst of vehement feeling from Gar. Kate has raised the most sensitive obstacle to Gar's leaving. If S.B. is going to miss him, why does he not say so? S.B.'s failure to communicate any sense of loss at Gar's departure is one of the central preoccupations of the play. Gar unleashes a tirade, not only against his inarticulate father, but against Ballybeg itself and its inhabitants: 'This place would drive anybody crazy! Look around you, for God's sake! . . . Asylum cases, the whole bloody lot of them!' This pronouncement has a hollow ring to it when we consider that throughout the play, Gar has been collecting 'memories and images and impressions' of the people in Ballybeg. He was deeply moved by Master Boyle's visit; he has distilled his memory of his exploits with 'the boys' and retained a 'precious memory'; and he has a deep-rooted, if unarticulated, affection for his father.

Gar is putting on a show: behind the cold, uncaring facade, lies a sensitive, emotional character. The language in this sequence is uncharacteristic of Gar and he seems to have adopted the vocabulary of Ned and Master Boyle. Gar denounces 'all this sentimental rubbish about "homeland" and "birthplace" ', echoing the phrases of Master Boyle: 'Impermanence — anonymity — that's what I'm looking for; a vast restless place that doesn't give a damn about the past. To hell with Ballybeg, that's what I say!' The irony of this speech is that the greater part of the play is taken up with aspects of life which Gar here vehemently denies: his search for memories that will be permanent, his struggle against anonymity and his need for friendship, love and communication.

In his farewell to Kate, Gar echoes Ned's parting words: 'And if you can't be good — you know?' After Kate's departure, Gar reveals his true personality. He is visibly shaken, buries his face in his hands and expresses his true feelings for Kate: 'Kate . . . sweet Katie Doogan . . . my darling Kathy Doogan . . .'. Private, in an attempt to restore Gar's sanity, quotes from Burke's *Reflections*. The quotation has the calming effect of incantation, and Gar is momentarily soothed. But immediately he is guilt ridden and frustrated. He realises that his love for Kate, who is now married, may be sinful, and he tries to cloud out her image by whistling *Philadelphia, Here I Come!* At this stage the dream of emigrating to America has lost much of its lustre. The 'vast restless place that doesn't give a damn about the past' is a frightening prospect against which Gar *must* retain some images and memories.

In a marvellous sequence where Friel uses the stream of consciousness technique to its full effect, Gar recalls incidents from the remote and recent past. Encapsulated between the memory of Gar's proposal to Kate and Kate's farewell are images of S.B., Madge and Master Boyle. Gar is revealed as a sad, isolated figure and his final whispered shout is a heart-rending appeal for a sign of love from the person that matters most to him: 'Screwballs, say something! Say something, father!'

EPISODE 3 — PART 1

Incantation and reverie

Madge, S.B., Public and Private are kneeling saying the rosary. As the 'monotonous, somnolent drone' continues in the background, Private begins to imagine his new life in America. Madge interrupts his fantasy and recalls him to say his decade of the rosary. Private and Public jump erect, and in perfect unison give out their decade. But gradually Gar's mind begins to wander again. Private moves over to S.B. He wonders if S.B. remembers the honeymoon in Bundoran and especially if he remembers an afternoon in May when father and son went fishing. After the rosary Madge goes to the kitchen to make supper and Gar tries to raise the subject of the fishing trip with his father. His efforts are thwarted by the entrance of Canon O'Byrne. (pp. 87-91)

COMMENTARY

THE opening of Episode 3 finds the O'Donnells and Madge saying the rosary. Gar's mind in not on the prayers and once again he fantasises about America. He pictures himself 'swaggering down 56th Street on Third at the junction of 29th and Seventh at 81st' with a blonde girl nuzzling up to him.

There are two points of interest here. Firstly, Gar displays an ignorance of the streets and avenues of Philadelphia. Anyone with even a passing knowledge of the organisation of streets in America would know that it is impossible to swagger down 56th Street on Third at the junction of 29th and Seventh at 81st — it simply defies logic.

Secondly, if we compare Gar's fantasy here with that of Ned's in the previous Episode we can see many points of similarity. Private has already informed us of the reality of the night when 'the boys' went out with

Gladys and Susan. There were no sexual conquests, no acts of daring — 'we straggled back home, one behind the other, and left the girls dangling their feet in the water'. But just as Public tries to keep alive the fantasies for Joe ('I'm telling you, you're missing the chance of a lifetime' p. 77), Private deludes himself with his own fantasies of America. Like Joe's realisation that Ned and Tom will only 'hang about the gable of the hotel and chat and do nothing', we suspect that Gar's fantasies will come to nothing.

The picture Private presents of Gar's future is a romantic version of S.B.'s life. He will be a silent, enigmatic bachelor until he is forty-three years old and then marry a beautiful young girl. It will be recalled that S.B. was in his forties when he married his nineteen-year-old bride.

The irony is that the more Gar criticises and finds faults with his father, the more he is becoming like his father. Overtly, he is silent and taciturn, 'a man of few words', and subconsciously his dreams and fantasies project a mirror image of his father. Madge's shrewd observation in the last scene of the play is already very close to the truth: 'And when he's (*Gar*) the age the boss is now, he'll turn out just the same'.

The recollection of the boating trip with his father reveals Gar's capacity for deep feeling and his longing for emotional communication. The details of the description and the vividness of the imagery are expressed in some of the most poetic and romantic language in the play:

> — do you remember — it was an afternoon in May — oh, fifteen years ago . . . the boat was blue and the paint was peeling and there was an empty cigarette packet floating in the water at the bottom between two trout and the left rowlock kept slipping and you had given me your hat and put your jacket round my shoulders because there had been a shower of rain . . . between us at that moment there was this great happiness, this great joy —you must have felt it too — it was so much richer than content — it was a great, great happiness, an active, bubbling joy — although nothing was being said — just the two of us fishing on a lake on a showery day . . . and then, then for no reason at all except that you were happy too, you began to sing . . . (pp. 89-90)

The great feeling of warmth and love reflected here is in sharp contrast to the indifferent, surly, taciturn behaviour of father and son in the reality of their everyday lives.

We have mentioned before how selective memory may distort one's recollections of the past. Gar so desperately wants to believe there *was* a 'great, great happiness', that it is possible he has exaggerated the whole description. We are to discover very shortly that S.B. has no recollection of the fishing trip. He does not recall the colour of the boat, or the song that was sung, so the accuracy of the description may be questioned. For a man like S.B. who weighs and measures facts, details are very important; for Gar, the colour of the boat or the name of the song is unimportant; what is important for him is that something happened which caused a great joy between father and son. The tragedy is that he cannot revive these emotions or resurrect the memory of the fishing trip in his father's mind.

Gar is so preoccupied with his thoughts that he is left kneeling when the others have finished their prayers. We get another glimpse of Madge's sardonic humour when she refers to the kneeling Gar as St. Martin de Porres: 'I suppose even the saints must eat now and again, too'. As Madge goes off to prepare supper, Gar and S.B. are alone together on stage. During the teatime sequence, Gar had listened to the ritual conversation of his father and mentally pleaded with him for some word or gesture of affection. Now, because time is running out, he tries to raise the subject of the fishing trip. S.B. has already started to dole out his ritual banalities: 'The days are shortening already. Before we know we'll be burning light before closing time'. With an extreme effort, prompted by Private's 'Go on! Ask him! He must remember!', Public asks in his churlish, off-hand tone: 'What ever happened to that aul boat on Lough na Cloc Cor?' S.B. mishears the question and Gar is forced to repeat it. At this most dramatic point, Canon O'Byrne interrupts the conversation. It is interesting to note that on the previous occasion when Gar and S.B. were alone, Master Boyle interrupted, destroying any hope that father and son had of talking on intimate terms.

Canon O'Byrne's visit

Canon O'Byrne enters for his nightly game of draughts with S.B. They play and talk as they do every other night, making only a scant reference to Gar's imminent departure. Private mimics the speech and gestures of the Canon. Madge brings in the supper and Public and Madge speak in hushed tones. Public encourages Madge to go and visit the Mulherns and see the new baby. He goes unnoticed to his bedroom while Private remains to mimic the draught players. Public puts on a record of Mendelssohn's violin concerto and Private interprets the music as reflecting the 'great beauty' that happened between Gar and S.B. on the fishing trip. S.B. and the Canon finally notice the music, but they continue with their game and their banal conversation. (pp. 91-9)

COMMENTARY

CANON O'Byrne is the last visitor to call to the O'Donnell house on the night before Gar's departure and it is significant that he, too, pays little attention to the fact that Gar is leaving. The Canon and S.B. are conspirators in the silence surrounding Gar's exile:

Canon: And how's the O'Donnell family tonight?

S.B.: Living away as usual. Not a thing happening.

Their failure to publicly recognise that this is an unusual night, that it is probably the most important night in Gar's life, causes Private to respond: 'Liar!'

The Canon and S.B. are cocooned in an atmosphere of easy familiarity and routine. One feels that they resent anything which disturbs the pattern of their set ways. Gar's proposed exile threatens the simple order of their lives: emigrating from Ballybeg could be seen as a rejection of the traditional social structure which gives authority to the Canon and the County Councillor. Ostensibly, Gar has no material reasons for emigrating.

He is the only son of a 'responsible, respectable citizen'. In the natural order of things he stands to inherit his father's grocery business. He is a dutiful son and, by Ballybeg standards, is well off. Turning his back on these things is an implied slight on the standards and expectations of the establishment. Rather than investigate the reasons for Gar's departure, the Canon and S.B., for the most part, ignore the fact that he is leaving.

'The boys' in a previous scene refused to acknowledge Gar's departure; they hid behind loud talk and bravado rather than admit any inadequacy in their own lives. In this scene, the Canon and S.B. give all their attention to their game of draughts; it takes on a significance far beyond the half-penny stakes. No interruptions are tolerated. The game is the shield which protects the participants from facing reality — it is the veil behind which they can hide and avoid serious discussion. When the Canon adverts to Gar's departure, S.B. ensures that a discussion about this topic will not develop:

Canon: It'll be getting near your time, Gareth.
Public: Tomorrow morning, Canon.
Canon: Just so, now. Tomorrow morning.
Private: Tomorrow morning.
Canon: Tomorrow morning.
S.B.:   Here we are.
Canon: Powerful the way time passes, too.

Here is the Canon's opportunity to 'say something', to make an 'unpredictable remark', to 'translate all this loneliness, this groping, this dreadful bloody buffoonery into Christian terms', but S.B. directs his attention back to the game: 'Black or white, Canon?'

Private is later to proclaim that 'there's an affinity between Screwballs and me that no one, literally, no one could understand', but there is also an affinity between 'Screwballs' and 'Canonballs' (to use Private's grotesque analogy). It is this affinity, perhaps, which will not allow any erosion or implied criticism of their social position. By ignoring Gar's departure, they are protecting their inheritance and preserving their authority.

The 'affinity' between the Canon and S.B. is highlighted by the interwoven pattern of their language. At the beginning of the scene the Canon uses the phrases 'Tomorrow morning', and 'Powerful the way time passes, too'. When the subject of Gar's departure is briefly mentioned at the end of the scene, it is S.B. who speaks these words: 'Aye, tomorrow morning. Powerful the way time passes, too'.

As S.B. and the Canon battle 'tooth and nail for another half-penny', Gar and Madge hold a hushed conversation, which begins with a mock attack on the draught-players who have shunted them into the background.

Madge: Wouldn't you love to throw it *(the cup of tea)* round them!
Public: Scalding hot!
Madge: And raise blisters on their aul bald pates! — God forgive me!

Here Madge and Gar speak like two schoolchildren, peevish at not being allowed to play with their elders. The tone of their conversation soon changes, however, and Gar reveals a sensitivity and concern for Madge. He encourages her to go and visit the new baby and he offers to 'put up the jars and wash up these few things'. At first, Madge is reluctant to go or to have Gar doing any extra chores, 'And this the last night we'll have you to torment us'. This unsolicited remark — a recognition of his impending exile — contrasts with the silence of the Canon and S.B.

Gar feels very close to Madge. Time and again she affirms her concern about his leaving. The warmth of their relationship at this point gives Gar courage to address a sensitive issue. As she goes to the scullery door he asks her: 'Why did my mother marry him *(S.B.)* instead of Master Boyle?' Madge, somewhat taken aback by the question, replies that Gar's mother 'married the better man by far' and if he has further questions, he should 'ask the Boss'. Not receiving a satisfactory answer to his question, Gar is angry with himself: 'What the hell had you to go and ask that for!' Public goes to his bedroom and Private stays to mimic the 'two dare-devils dicing with death' over a game of draughts. In a sustained monologue, Private appeals to the Canon and to S.B. for a show of affection. 'Tell me, boys, strictly between ourselves, will you miss me? You will? You really will?' It is ironic that Private is here echoing the words that Public used when talking to Madge in the opening sequence of the play. The irony is that Public can articulate his need for love and affirmation to Madge, but in the presence of his father it is the silent voice of Private that calls for a show of affection: the voice of his inner thoughts goes unheard and unheeded.

The mimicry and humour of Private's antics change to an emotional cry from the heart as Public plays the Mendelssohn record. When the music begins, Private rushes to the table, thrusts his head between the two players and says:

Listen! Listen! Listen! D'you hear it? D'you know what the music says? *(To S.B.)* It says that once upon a time a boy and his father sat in a blue boat on a lake on an afternoon in May, and on that afternoon a great beauty happened, a beauty that has haunted the boy ever since, because he wonders now did it really take place or did he imagine it. There are only the two of us, he says; each of us is all the other has; and why can we not even look at each other? Have pity on us, he says; have goddam pity on every goddam bloody man jack of us . . . To hell with all strong silent men!

Gar's hopes that the music would arouse some reaction in the players is dashed and S.B. and the Canon end the scene speaking almost in unison, secure in their parochial existence, blind to the pathos of Gar's vigil in Ballybeg.

EPISODE 3 — PART 2

Gar and S.B.

*Gar, lying in his bedroom, hears a noise. He thinks it is
Madge bolting the door. Private reminds him that he has only
four more hours before his departure. He goes to get a packet of
aspirin from the shop and he is startled to meet S.B. in the
kitchen. They begin to talk about the affairs of the shop and S.B.
briefly mentions Gar's travel arrangements. Gar re-introduces his
recollection of the fishing-trip, but S.B. does not recall the
incident. Gar, disillusioned, rushes quickly to the shop. S.B. is left
alone in the kitchen. (pp. 100-6)*

COMMENTARY

THIS is the final meeting of Gar and S.B. in the play. It is their last
chance for real communication. We are becoming more aware of the
affect Gar's departure is having on S.B. Here Friel creates a clever
juxtaposition of father and son engaged in the same activity — collecting
memories and images of the past. In the kitchen, S.B. looks at Gar's packed
cases. He touches his son's coat, then he sits and stares at the bedroom door.
In the bedroom, Gar is collecting images and impressions. He sits on the
edge of the bed and looks at the familiar objects around him, knowing that
he may be looking at them for the last time. His mind is like a camera which
will capture and store these familiar images. Private in his final speech
reinforces the idea of the mind as camera: 'keep the camera whirring; for
this is a film you'll run over and over again' (p. 110). Because Gar has only
four more hours to spend in the house, familiar objects are no longer taken
for granted — they assume a special significance: 'Four more hours. This is
the last time you'll lie in this bed, the last time you'll look at the pattern *(on
the floor),* the last time you'll listen to the silence of Ballybeg . . .'

In order to help him get back to sleep, Gar goes to get a packet of

47

aspirin from the shop. He is startled to find his father in the kitchen. Just as Gar is taciturn and quiet in the presence of his elders, S.B. is hesitant and unsure when speaking to his son. He stammers a halting explanation for being awake in the small hours of the morning. Earlier, at tea-time, Gar was prepared to let the 'silent' voice of Private plead on his behalf for a word or gesture of affection from his father. Here, however, time is running out for Gar. He has to take the initiative. The last words S.B. spoke to Gar at teatime were: 'Sure you know I never take a second cup'. After this remark, Private accepted that no further conversation could be conducted between them. Here, when S.B. restates the banal response, Gar Private makes a further effort to continue the conversation between them:

> Playing hard to get. Come on, bucko; it's your place to make the move — the younger man. Say — say — say — say 'Screwballs, with two magnificent legs like that, how is it you were never in show biz?' Say, 'It is now sixteen or seventeen —' — Say — oh my God — say — say something.

Here Private is exhorting Public to make an 'unpredictable remark', to say something that will communicate his affection for his father. This plea is reminiscent of Private's plea to S.B. in the tea-time sequence when he said:

> So now, Screwballs, say . . . *(thinks)* . . .
> 'Once upon a time a rainbow ended in our garden' . . . say, 'I like to walk across the White Strand when there's a misty rain falling' . . . say, 'Gar, son —' say, 'Gar, you bugger you, why don't you stick it out here with me for it's not such a bad aul bugger of a place'. Go on. Say it! Say it! Say it! (pp. 40-41)

What S.B. actually said on that occasion is far from the poetic heights that Gar imagined. He said: 'I didn't find as many *(rats)* about the year'. Now, when Public is asked to say something meaningful, to make an 'unpredictable remark' he comes out with: 'You'll need a new tyre for the van.'

Public and S.B. remain on safe ground. They talk about what they are most familiar with — the shop. Tyres, fencing posts, pliars, tea-chests, plug tobacco, tin cans and kettles, each in turn is mentioned or discussed. At the first hint of a break in the conversation, Private encourages Public to continue: 'You're doing grand. Keep at it. It's the silence that's the enemy'. This is an echo of Friel's stage direction concerning 'the boys': 'Tranquility is their enemy: they fight it valiantly' (p. 68). S.B. and Gar talk and list items concerning the shop until, finally, their real feelings emerge. S.B., rambling on about the number of tin cans he used to sell before the popular use of cookers and ranges, says: 'All cans it was then. Maybe you'd sell a kettle at turf-cutting or if there'd be a Yank coming home . . .'. America is on S.B.'s mind and he cannot hide his concern about Gar's departure. For the first time in the play, he addresses his remarks to the details of Gar's travel arrangements. We learn that he has been listening to the weather forecast:

> S.B.: I was thinking it — it — it — it would be a fair
> enough day for going up in thon plane.
> Public: It should be, then.
> S.B.: Showers — just like the Canon said . . . And I was
> meaning to tell you that you should sit at the back . . .
> Private: It is now sixteen or seventeen years — the longest
> way round's the shortest way home —
> S.B.: So *he* was saying, too . . . you know there — if there
> was an accident or anything — it's the front gets it
> hardest —
> Public: I suppose that's true enough.
> S.B.: So *he* was saying . . . not that I would know — just
> that he was saying it there . . .

S.B. gives this simple, even pathetic, advice about where to sit on the plane, but he does not accept full responsibility for his own remarks. He is at pains to attribute the advice to the Canon. This shows S.B.'s self-consciousness and insecurity — he has not the confidence to offer his son advice.

Private, sensing that his father might be in a sentimental, reminiscent mood, tries once again to talk about the afternoon in May when the 'great happiness' was experienced between father and son on the fishing trip. To his dismay, he finds that S.B. is more concerned with the details of the event, rather than with the event itself. Gar desperately wants his father to remember the afternoon of the fishing trip — it is his last chance to prove to himself that there *is* an 'affinity' between father and son: that S.B. and Gar are capable of sharing a great emotional happiness:

> Public: D'you remember the blue boat?
> S.B.: A blue one, eh?
> Public: I don't know who owned it. But it was blue. And the
> paint was peeling.
> S.B.: *(remembering)* I mind a brown one the doctor
> brought from somewhere up in the —

Public: *(quickly)* It doesn't matter who owned it. It doesn't even
matter that it was blue. But d'you remember one afternoon
in May — we were up there — the two of us — and it must
have rained because you put your jacket round my
shoulders and gave me your hat —

S.B.:   Aye?

Public: — and it wasn't that we were talking or anything — but
suddenly — suddenly you sang 'All Round My Hat I'll
Wear a Green Coloured Ribbono' —

S.B.:   Me?

Public: — for no reason at all except that we — that you were
happy. D'you remember? D'you remember? *(There is a
pause while S.B. tries to recall.)*

S.B.:   No . . . no, then, I don't . . .

Gar is deflated. Private taunts him by saying: 'So now you know: it
never happened! Ha-ha-ha-ha-ha.' Public has shrouded his memory with
emotion. He attaches too much importance to a little incident; the fact that
S.B. cannot remember it, does not necessarily mean that the incident never
happened. Once again, memory is seen to be illusive. Ned's recollection of
being out with Annie McFadden is distorted; Aunt Lizzy has faulty
recollections of dates and events; in the next scene S.B. recalls Gar being
dressed in a sailor-suit but Madge says that Gar never had a sailor-suit; and
here the fishing-trip, the colour of the boat and the title of the song are
called into question.

Gar rushes out and S.B. is left alone, weighing and measuring the
facts. 'In the dead early hours, the remembered open prospects of the past
recede; may, indeed, never have been.' (D. E. S. Maxwell).

A boy in a sailor-suit

Madge returns from her visit to the Mulhern family. She finds S.B. alone in the kitchen. She tells him that her grandniece is going to be called Brigid. S.B. does not realise how much this affects Madge. He tells Madge about Gar as a young boy going to school dressed in a sailor-suit. Madge does not recall the incident or the sailor-suit. (pp. 106-8)

COMMENTARY

MADGE'S private disappointment is revealed here. Earlier in the play she had told Gar with 'shy delight' about the birth of her grandniece: 'And they're going to call this one Madge — at least so she *says*' (p. 37). Now Madge returns from her visit to the Mulhern household, sad and very weary, and she tells S.B. that the baby is going to be called Brigid. S.B., unaware of her defeated hopes, fails to see that Madge is extremely disappointed: 'Brigid — that's a grand name . . . Patrick, Brigid, and Colmcille . . .'. Had Madge revealed her disappointment to Gar he would have responded in a more sympathetic and comforting way. However, Madge hides the knowledge of the new baby's name from the one person who may have responded or understood her distress.

Madge's failure to reveal her private experience to the right person is cleverly juxtaposed (or paralleled) by S.B.'s revelation to Madge of the sailor-suit incident. Here, in the final appearance of S.B. on stage, Friel gives us our deepest insight into his character. Up to this point, S.B. has displayed his emotions more by actions and gestures than by speech. Here, however, we see that S.B. has an emotional side to his character. This scene answers Private's earlier question:

> God — maybe — Screwballs — behind those dead eyes and that flat face are there memories of precious moments in the past? (p. 89)

This short sequence is filled with irony. It follows Gar's attempt to share a precious memory with his father, and Madge's failure to communicate her disappointment. S.B. does not remember the fishing trip with Gar, but he has his memories of the past. The irony here is that S.B. shares his memory with Madge rather than with Gar. And Madge shares her sense of disappointment with S.B.

S.B. describes to Madge his remembered moment of great happiness — how father and son walked to school 'the two of us, hand in hand, as happy as larks — we were that happy, Madge — and him dancing and chatting beside me — mind? — you couldn't get a word in edge-ways with all the chatting he used to go through . . .'. S.B. is echoing Madge's words, when she ironically commented on the silence between father and son during the tea-time scene: 'A body couldn't get a word in edgeways with you two!' (p. 42).

Madge is left to console S.B. He wonders if the lack of communication between himself and his son was due to the fact that he married a woman far younger than himself:

> S.B.:   . . . Maybe, Madge, maybe it's because I could have
>   been his grandfather, eh?
> Madge: I don't know.
> S.B.:   I was too old for her, Madge, eh?
> Madge: I don't know. They're a new race — a new world.
> S.B.:   *(leaving)* In the wee sailor suit . . . I don't know
>   either . . .

The repetition of the phrase 'I don't know' by Madge and S.B. anticipates Gar's final words in the play: 'I don't know. I — I — I don't know.'

Finale

Madge, in a weary soliloquy, talks about the name for the new baby and expresses concern for the future welfare of Gar. She puts money in an envelope and slips the envelope into his coat pocket. Public returns from the shop and he and Madge talk. As Madge slowly shuffles off, Private tries to retain the memory of his last image of her. Gar goes to his room asking the agonising question: 'God, Boy, why do you have to leave? Why? Why?' (pp. 108-10)

COMMENTARY

THE *finale* puts many earlier events into perspective. Friel uses a technique of internal monologue here: Madge talking to herself, reviews the events of the play. This technique is similar to the soliloquy of classical drama, but it allows for a freer association of ideas; hence the punctuation, with many dots and dashes, showing mental changes and the shifting from one idea to another: 'Brigid — Biddy — Biddy Mulhern — Brigid Mulhern — aye — like Madge Mulhern doesn't sound right — *(Trying it out)* — Madge Mulhern — Madge Mulhern — I don't know — it's too aul'-fashioned or something . . . Has he his cap?'

Because Madge is speaking to herself, speaking aloud, this review of events is detached and dispassionate. It reveals Madge as being sharply observant, thoughtful, wise and knowledgeable about the world: 'Tomorrow'll be sore on him *(Gar):* his heart'll break tomorrow, and all next week, and the week after maybe . . .'. Madge realises that the leaving will be difficult for Gar, but she also implies that the sorrow of exile will be only a temporary emotion. In this she is echoing Master Boyle's reservations about Gar's continuing loyalty to Ballybeg and its inhabitants:

> Boyle: Perhaps you'll write me.
> Public: I will indeed.
> Boyle: Yes, the first year. Maybe the second . . . (p. 47)

There is an element in Madge's monologue of the older woman smiling at the vagaries of youth. Finding an apple in Gar's coat pocket she remarks: '. . . an apple, if you don't mind — for all his grief. He'll be all right.' This wry comment brings a degree of humour and realism to Gar's departure: it is not as tragic as he might wish to believe. Madge is a realist. She accepts life, and the world, as it is presented to her. Sorrow is a natural part of exile, but it is not a permanent malaise. As Gar gets established in Philadelphia, his anguish and sorrow will fade. This knowledge of the ways of the world doesn't make Madge hard-hearted — she doesn't mock Gar's emotions and she deliberately tries to make the parting as painless as possible. Unlike Boyle, there is no envy in her at Gar's opportunity to go to America although her own life is restricted in many ways. Her remark that 'there's no big dances between now and then' is an ironic comment on her own situation.

Madge is sceptical of Lizzy's material possessions ('I'll believe them things when I see them!') yet she acknowledges her ability to take care of Gar. This healthy scepticism allows Madge to accept her world, unlike Boyle who cannot come to terms with his. He is frustrated and disappointed with his lot. Friel is here highlighting the paradox of social position: on the one hand the Master, traditionally renowned for his learning and status in society, is unable to find personal fulfilment or establish a satisfactory identity; on the other hand Madge, who is a 'mere housekeeper', a woman in a patriarchal society, has the confidence to be outspoken, accepts her position in society and is revealed as being worldly and wise.

Our impression of Madge's wisdom and self-assurance is enhanced by her gesture of raising her hand 'in a sort of vague Benediction', before she delivers her most pointed comment on Gar and S.B. Here she assumes an almost priestly authority in ironic contrast to Canon O'Byrne's inability to 'translate all this loneliness, this groping, this dreadful bloody buffoonery into Christian terms that will make life bearable for us all'. Madge's comment on Gar and S.B. places the 'loneliness' and 'buffoonery' in the context of the shared characteristics of father and son: 'as like as two peas. And when he's *(Gar)* the age the boss is now, he'll turn out just the same'.

In the final exchanges between Public and Madge each attempts to speak with consideration for the other's concerns. Yet neither is willing to directly address those matters which concern them most. Not for the first time in the play, when important issues need to be discussed the conversation switches to routine affairs:

Madge: The jars are up?
Public: They are.
Madge: And the dishes washed?
Public: All done.

As the play comes to a close they imbue their ordinary words with as much affection as they can:

Madge: Good night.
Public: Sleep well, Madge.
Madge: Sleep well yourself.

This final sequence is an affirmation of the ordinary and common nature of the conflict in Gar's soul. His speech is no longer bawdy and raucous. 'Screwballs' of the earlier scenes is now referred to with concern, affection and dignity: 'Madge — Madge, you'd let me know if — if he got sick or anything?' In simple language Gar expresses his concern for his father. While there is confusion at the end of the play, Gar's 'I don't know. I — I — I don't know' is almost his way of saying 'I *do* know that I love these people'. The final scene ends with a sense of affirmation or redemption. For all their failings and weaknesses, the humanity of the characters comes through. It is a lyrical scene, and the lyricism gives a gloss to the earlier episodes in the play. Pretence, exaggeration and buffoonery give way at last to gentle concern, caring and humanity.

This type of *finale* is consistent with Friel's ideas on the function of dramatists. 'They are not marriage counsellors, nor father confessors, nor politicians, nor economists. What function have they, then? They have this function: they are vitally, persistently, and determinedly concerned with one man's insignificant place in the here-and-now world. They have the function to portray that one man's frustrations and hopes and anguishes and joys and miseries and pleasures with all the precision and accuracy and truth that they know; and by so doing help to make a community of individuals . . . And when they depict in mean, gruesome detail only one portion of our existence, perhaps in this generation the dominant portion, they are crying out for recognition of the existence of something less ignoble, something more worthy. They are asking us to recognise that even in confusion and disillusion, strength and courage can exist, and that out of them can come a redemption of the human spirit.' (*The Theatre of Hope and Despair*)

Friel presents the problem of Gar's exile as the problem of his youthfulness — he has to leave home in order to grow up. He is a decent person, but our hearts will not break for him; we will end up smiling at him, rather than regarding him as a tragic hero. The *New Yorker* review of *Philadelphia, Here I Come!* summarised the basic nature of the play thus: *(Philadelphia)* 'is concerned with the dilemma of a romantic young resident of an Irish town called Ballybeg who, after deciding to leave his bleak native heath for what he imagines to be the excitements of Philadelphia, is afflicted on the night before his departure with urgent doubts as to whether he is making a sensible move. While this might seem to boil down to nothing more important than the problem outlined by Jimmy Durante when he sang "Did you ever have that feeling that you wanted to go, and yet that you wanted to stay?" Mr. Friel presents the question with a nice appreciation of the quandary of a young man well aware of the frustrations of his parochial existence but also reluctantly conscious of the fact that Philadelphia may not prove the Shangri-La of his reckless daydreams.'

In the final analysis, the issues raised in the play — lack of communication (S.B. and Gar); disappointment and failure (the three marriages); social class consciousness (Senator Doogan); frustration (Master Boyle); and inadequacy (Canon O'Byrne) — all these are more important and more agonising than Gar's predicament, the predicament of a young man leaving home.

The Themes

IN *Philadelphia Here I Come!* Brian Friel explores the spiritual impoverishment of life in a small town in rural Ireland. The play is expressly concerned with failure and inadequacy at almost every human level: personal, social, sexual, emotional and imaginative.

The central character, Gar O'Donnell, on the eve of his departure to America, can see these inadequacies operating in his own life, but lacks the personal resources and maturity to overcome them. In recognising the sterility of life in Ballybeg, Gar hungers for fulfilment — the emotional fulfilment of being loved by his father and affirmed in that love, the sexual fulfilment of a viable relationship with a young woman and the imaginative fulfilment of creating a life for himself beyond the narrow confines of his home town. Gar's greatest failure, however, is his inability to address those matters which most concern him — his problematic love for his father, his failure in college, his disappointment in love and his ambiguous feelings for his native place. Gar poses as a buffoon and exchanges a glib loquacity for real speech. His 'eejiting about' marks a heart-felt loneliness and a keen sense of his own inadequacy. His pathetic timidity and subsequent failure to achieve a dignified sense of self in the interview with Senator Doogan, is an utter humiliation for Gar.

Thereafter, he seeks the means to escape the constricting circumstances of his environment. Aunt Lizzy's invitation to Philadelphia offers a way out of Ballybeg, but is hardly a true opportunity for freedom. Gar trades his father's infuriating silence for the mothering sentimentality of his Aunt Lizzy. The final irony of the play is that Gar's repudiation of home and family ('I hate the place . . . hate it! hate it!'), separates him from the people and the place that mean most to him in the world. However curtailed the possibilities of life in Ballybeg are, Gar is among those he loves, notwithstanding his inability to voice his feelings for them. Neither the America of his fantasies, nor the crass materialism of Lizzy will feed Gar's spiritual and emotional hunger. In the early morning of his departure, Gar questions why he has to leave, and cannot find a satisfactory answer. The curtain falls on Gar's confusion and uncertainty.

 1 Failure and fantasy

BALLYBEG is a small community inhabiting a small world. The pattern of life is set and predictable. At the end of a day's work, Gar can anticipate his father's every word and gesture:

> Private: Repeat slowly after me: Another day over.
> S.B.:   Another day over.
> Private: Good. Next phrase. I suppose we can't complain.
> S.B.:   I suppose we can't complain. (p. 39)

Even on Gar's last evening at home, S.B. cannot alter the habit and routine of long years. Madge, conscious that Gar is eager for some word or act of love, speaks out to S.B. and, in doing so, signals her own frustration at the habitual reticence of S.B. Gar is wounded by his father's silence, and he seeks a release from his disappointment in a series of confused fantasies, which he acts out in an exaggerated and verbose manner. His frustration is mirrored in his intemperate speech: 'and then away down below in the Atlantic you see a bloody bugger of an Irish boat out fishing for bloody pollock . . . (p. 17). This escape, however, lacks any imaginative richness. Ger rehearses a series of stereotyped attitudes in a language that is cliché-ridden and second-hand. The Philadelphia of his imagination is the Philadelphia of the American dream — with hard work Gar O'Donnell can make it to the very top, can become 'president of the biggest chain of biggest hotels in the world' (p. 22). His other fantasies are equally unreal and adolescent — Gareth O'Donnell, the virtuoso conductor and violinist; Gar O'Donnell, the pride of the Ballybeg team with 'magic in his feet'!

There is a marked difference in tone when Gar addresses his mind to the lived experience of his family, or recalls Madge's description of his mother. In those moments, Gar Private speaks a language that is infused with emotion and intensity:

> She was small, Madge says, and wild, and young, Madge says, from a place called Bailtefree beyond the mountains; and her eyes were bright, and her hair was loose . . . (p. 25)

Gar, however, cannot cope with the powerful feeling he experiences in relation to his mother. He quells the rising tide of emotion by uttering the ritual prayers for the dead, and finally blots out his private meditation by reciting aloud lines from Burke's *Reflections on the Revolution in France*, which he employs as a means of controlling his agitation. Immediately following this episode, he launches into an energetic bout of 'eejiting about'. This is an extremely important scene in helping us to read Gar's character. In it we recognise Gar's failure to confront the emotions released by his deeper self. The ego and the id speak in competing voices, but the id ultimately shouts itself down for fear of the feelings and the painful reality rendered up from Gar's store of memory. When Gar acts the buffoon, or recites a litany of abuse against his father, he is in control, and chooses the character he will portray and the voice in which he will speak. But the id, Private, can lead Gar into areas of his existence that he would prefer to avoid. On two occasions Gar's inner feelings break through his self-imposed limits, infusing the quotation from Burke's *Reflections on the Revolution in France* with the painful emotion of his inner self, and transforms a formula for controlling his emotions into a cry of pain.

> . . . and maybe it was good of God to take her away three days after you were born . . . *(Suddenly boisterous.)* Damn you, anyhow, for a bloody stupid bastard! It is now sixteen or seventeen years since I saw the Queen of France, then the Dauphiness, at Versailles! (pp. 25-6)

Similarly, when Kate Doogan calls to say goodbye, Gar is overcome by a rush of emotion. Private attempts to contain this by reciting the quotation from Burke, but the words take their meaning from Gar's love for Kate, and refer as much to Kate as to 'Marie Antoinette'.

Oh my God, steady man, steady — it is now sixteen or
seventeen years since I saw the Queen of France, then the
Dauphiness, at Versailles, and surely never lighted on this
orb — Oh God, Oh my God, those thoughts are sinful —
(p. 82)

On one further occasion Gar's speech assumes a note of authenticity
and longing. His accusation that the Canon, and, by implication, the
Catholic Church, has failed to offer Gar, and the community to which he
belongs, a reading of their lives that makes sense of 'all this loneliness, this
groping, this dreadful bloody buffoonery', is an acknowledgement of the
impoverished state of his existence. Paradoxically, in the admission of his
frailty, Gar achieves a dignity. Haltingly, and hesitantly, Gar moves on to
recall the most painful and beautiful of his memories, 'a blue boat on a lake
on an afternoon in May, and on that afternoon a great beauty happened . . .'
(p. 98). If this memory contains any emotional truth that his father can
share, then Gar's longing and need to belong and be loved will be satisfied.
Summoning all his courage, Gar calls the memory to S.B.'s mind. S.B., too
long accustomed to measuring and weighing, searches out the facts and
accuracy of the memory, and misses its significance. For Gar, the moment
has passed, and he withdraws in a confusion of self-mockery. The failure
here is not Gar's or S.B.'s personally, but the failure of a community that is
customarily reticent on matters of love and affection. Although S.B. is
trapped in his empirical way of thinking and cannot respond in kind to Gar,
he too possesses a memory of happier times. However, it is with Madge that
he shares it. In this instance, it is she who questions the objective truth of
the memory.

Memory as depicted in the play, is a creative faculty, recreating the
images of the past in order to preserve the significant moments in a person's
life. The subjective and emotional truth of a memory is as important to the
individual as the factual status of the events remembered. The irony for
S.B. is that he chooses to share his memory with Madge. Had it been shared
with Gar, then Gar might have been confirmed in his earlier intuition that
'behind those dead eyes and that flat face are there memories of precious
moments in the past?' (p. 89). By the end of the play, both Gar and S.B. have
spoken in vivid and moving terms of their love, each for the other, a love
locked firmly in the past, and which neither is capable of hauling into the
present. We are left with the impression of a failure to speak their love, not
of love's absence.

Gar's immaturity is most clearly evident in the episode with Kate and her father. In this instance Gar's failure to achieve a mature, personal identity costs him dearly. Gar's love for Kate is a mixture of adolescent escapism and sexual desire. He tells Kate that he will 'burst', he will 'never last till Easter'. Their sons will be 'sexy goats', and their daughters 'frail, gentle and silly'. Kate, for her part, displays a surer grasp of social and financial realities. She is conscious of the material and social considerations that govern the choice of a marriage partner, and realises that her father will not give consent to her marrying someone with an income of £3 15s per week. Consequently, Kate rehearses Gar in a fiction that will prove acceptable to her father: 'You have £20 a week and £5,000 in the bank and your father's about to retire' (p. 31). As she leaves Gar to speak to the Senator, she reminds him that their future is in his hands. Gar fails, however, to act maturely and cannot translate his childish daydreams into adult reality. He offers no resistance to Doogan's talk of 'old friends' and 'school acquaintances' nor to the prospect of a match between Francis King and Kate. Unwilling to acknowledge his self-betrayal, in a fit of peevishness, Gar blames Kate.

The visit of 'the boys' highlights another aspect of the impoverished life of Ballybeg and describes another form of fantasy. 'The boys' do not refer to Gar's imminent departure, fearful lest it throw into stark perspective their own bleak future. Instead they boast of countless seductions and sexual conquests and in the process create for themselves the illusion of virility and experience. They feign an air of bravado and nonchalance. But here, as in the plays of O'Casey, their endless talk serves only to deflect their listeners from the fact that they have nothing to say. There is about them a superficial and comic vitality, but this cannot obscure the emptiness of their lives and their incapacity to overcome it. They leave Gar to pursue a further 'adventure'. Joe, the youngest of the trio describes the reality of what lies in store: 'Sure you know yourself they'll hang about the gable of the hotel and chat and do nothing' (p. 77).

Their visit creates a conflict in Gar. He has already attained a detachment from 'the boys', and can recognise the self-deception in their bravado, the falseness of the aggressive masculine image they project. Wearily, he contrasts the fantasy of their stories with the reality. Ned's awkward gesture of friendship stirs old loyalties, but these are shaken when he learns that his friends have not come of their own accord. Desperately, Private searches for something he can cling to, something that will give validation to his friendship with 'the boys' over the years:

> '. . . for there *was* fun and there *was* laughing — foolish, silly fun and
> foolish, silly laughing, but what it was all about you can't remember,
> can you? Just the memory of it — that's all you have now — just the
> memory; and even now, even so soon, it is being distilled of its
> coarseness; and what's left is going to be precious, precious gold . . .'.
> (pp. 78-9)

Gar is here speaking to convince himself. Memory and rhetoric combine to create a new fantasy. His life in Ballybeg is deliberately surrendered to the softening and idealising power of memory.

Lizzy has already broken away from Ballybeg. When she returns she is brash, vulgar and superior in her attitude to those who have remained. She too speaks endlessly, hardly pausing for breath. In many respects Liz is like 'the boys' and Gar. She hides the suffering and emptiness of her life behind a flow of eloquence. She tells Gar that America is 'Gawd's own country'. Ben Burton speaks nearer the truth with his reply that 'It's just another place to live, Elise. Ireland — America — what's the difference?' (p. 62). The clearest and most pitiful insight we obtain into Lizzy's character occurs when she numbers herself among the dead Gallagher girls. For Lizzy, life has been a kind of death. She has no children, a failure which wounds her deeply. She is married to a man to whom she shows few signs of affection or love. Even when she speaks out of her great need and anguish, her voice cannot free itself from self-pity and cloying sentimentality.

Reviewing the play, one cannot but be struck by the repeated failure of characters to achieve a stable and fulfilled life. In rare moments of insight or self-pity, they acknowledge their failures, but for the most part they create fantasies into which they escape from the futility of their lives. It is this sense of futility, and our identification with their longings for love and fulfilment which makes the play a tragic statement, despite the wonderful moments of comedy and farce.

2 Love and disappointment

DISAPPOINTMENT is an integral part of the experience of life in Ballybeg. Nowhere is this more evident than in the play's treatment of love and marriage. In an obvious way the male characters (Gar, S.B. and Boyle) are disappointed in love, but it is the experience of the female characters (Kate, Lizzy, Maire and Madge), that provides the richest source of dramatic insight. The women are subject to the accepted conventions and attitudes of male society. The boys' (and Gar) reveal some of society's attitudes to women. Women are there to satisfy the sexual desires of the male, or, as in the case of Madge, to attend and give emotional support to the self-centred male. Kate, as a woman, is not free to choose whom she will marry. Her position is one of passivity. However alert she is to the social realities, she cannot engage or alter those realities, or subvert the social and material criteria employed in the selection of a 'suitable' husband. Kate is not alone in this. Maire was married to a man twenty-one years her senior, because he had 'a big store', and though Lizzy tells us that S.B. was good to her, the marriage was not a love match. In Lizzy's case, her feelings for Con are ambiguous. Her 'love' for him is distorted. She constantly makes little of him and pays much attention to Ben Burton, although there is no question of sexual involvement. Lizzy is a self-professed Catholic. Her years in America have given her a brash vulgarity, but have not robbed her of a sense of the absolute nature of the marriage contract. When Lizzy breaks down, Ben Burton leaves the room, indicating his unwillingness to intrude in the private world of Con and Lizzy's marriage.

The exploration of marriage may be read and interpreted in the light of de Valera's constitution, which was enacted in 1937, the year of S.B. and Maire's marriage. The coincidence of dates draws attention to the central place ascribed to marriage and family life in that document, and then forces the audience to distinguish between the rhetoric of the new Ireland and the social reality.

The scene of Lizzy's visit brings the three marriages (S.B. and Maire, Lizzy and Con, Kate and Francis King) into focus. The visit occurs on

Kate's wedding day, and Lizzy spends most of the time recalling Maire's marriage to S.B. All three marriages share and repeat a pattern of disappointment. As Lizzy talks on, the sense of the past being renewed in the present is evident in the blending of the three marriages. Each story is interwoven with the others, to the point of telling the one tale. A most dramatic moment in the scene occurs when Lizzy includes herself among the dead members of the family. The desolation implicit in this statement might well serve to characterise the experience of marriage for the three women. Their lives have not been redeemed by the presence of love.

Lizzy's trip to Ireland is a pilgrimage of hope. She looks on Gar as a source of consolation. He might lessen the emptiness of her life. He is someone upon whom she can lavish affection. Her desperate longing for a child reveals itself when she claims Gar as her son. This claim is a fantasy, but one that partially satisfies Lizzy's longing for a child. For many people children give meaning and a sense of completion to their lives. The absence of children is experienced as a perceptible loss. Paradoxically, S.B., whom Gar wishes to be his father in act and speech, cannot assume his fatherly role, and it is Gar who feels the sense of loss. Boyle, who could have been Gar's father, demonstrates a real affection for Gar, when he comes to bid him farewell. Gar's resolution to leave is shaken by this incident, and his need for love and affirmation, as well as his emotional loyalty to Ballybeg, is clearly revealed. This loyalty makes his bid for freedom a source of pain and conflict.

Madge's life is also marked by disappointment. In many respects, she has the strongest claim on Gar's love, but she does not force this upon him. She is warm and motherly in her care of him. Her love is both kind and practical. On the eve of his departure she lays out his clothes, invites his friends to tea, and secretly places two pounds in his coat-pocket. She is both nurse and mother to him, and someone in whom he can confide. For his part, Gar takes Madge largely for granted and rarely demonstrates his affection for her. Saddened that her sister's child has not been called after her, as was promised, Madge expresses something of her disappointment with life: 'I'm just tired, son. Very tired' (p. 109). The form of address hints at her own feelings for Gar. So too does her hostile reaction to Lizzy. It might be reasonable to suppose that Madge's antipathy to Lizzy is motivated by her intuition of Lizzy's rivalry for 'her' son. It is significant that the play ends with Gar's recognition of his love for Madge. It is a valuable insight, but one that comes too late for both of them.

3 Exile, freedom and the past

PHILADELPHIA, Here I Come! is a drama of exile, Gar's exile. However, Gar's departure to America is not forced upon him by economic necessity. The impoverishment of his life in Ballybeg is not that of material deprivation. Gar is a spiritual exile. He is already dislocated from his family and friends before his departure for America. Thus he refers to his father as 'Screwballs! Skinflint! Skittery Face' (p. 20). His friends appear tedious and juvenile: 'The boys . . . They weren't always like this, were they?' (p. 71). Ballybeg is 'a bloody quagmire, a backwater, a dead end!' (p. 81).

It is to escape the impoverishment of Ballybeg and to achieve a degree of freedom that Gar accepts Lizzy's invitation to Philadelphia. Once accepted, however, Gar becomes conscious of a fidelity to his native place and of his strong emotional ties to those around him. This is the central conflict of the play — the urge to freedom opposing the love of one's native place. In the farewell scene with Kate, Gar Public dismisses his loyalties with a show of aggression:

> Answerable to nobody! All this bloody yap about father and son and all this sentimental rubbish about 'homeland' and 'birthplace' — yap! Bloody yap! . . . To hell with Ballybeg, that's what I say! (p. 81)

But these sentiments belie his true state of mind. The decision to depart is, in many respects, a dramatic gesture, aimed at overcoming the reluctance of father and son to express their love for each other. Up to the hours before his departure, Gar hopes for a sign, gesture, or act of love from his father:

> So tonight d'you know what I want you to do? I want you to make one unpredictable remark . . . say, 'Gar son —' say, 'Gar, you bugger you, why don't you stick it out here with me for it's not such a bad aul bugger of a place.' Go on. Say it! Say it! Say it! (pp. 40-1)

Gar's plans for departure fail to overcome the silence between him and his father. At moments in the play Gar comes close to conceding that love cannot be expressed or acknowledged, that real communication is impossible between those who are closest to each other. This fatalism is especially evident in Gar's comment, 'It doesn't matter. Forget it.' (p. 105), coming, as it does, after Gar's most sustained and earnest attempt to speak meaningfully to his father.

Allied to Gar's sense of isolation is his search for an identity and his need to escape from the domination of the past. Master Boyle, S.B., Senator Doogan and the Canon represent the range of possible futures for Ballybeg's young generation — teacher, shopkeeper, politician or clergyman. Gar rejects all of these possibilities. Philadelphia offers a new set of possibilities, notwithstanding the shallow and vulgar nature of the life recounted by Lizzy.

Philadelphia symbolises the future; Ballybeg represents an inescapable past which Gar attempts to interpret and make sense of. When Gar lays down his clown's mask, he invariably dwells on a past which cannot be recaptured, but which refuses to yield to the present. Gar's most insistent and intense questions address the past:

> Private: ... And he must have known, old Screwballs,
>   he must have known, Madge says, for many a
>   night he must have heard her crying herself
>   to sleep ... (p. 25)
>
> Private: And Maire, my mother, did you love her?
>   (p. 45)
>
> Public: Why did my mother marry him *(S.B.)* instead
>   of Master Boyle? (p. 94)
>
> Public: *(to S.B.)* There used to be a blue boat on it — d'you
>   remember it? (p. 104)

Philadelphia represents an opportunity to break free of this insistent past. Philadelphia is the future, albeit one that does not inspire, or command our regard. Gar stores up memories to carry with him. Deliberately, he surrenders his past to memory, the most sentimental and selective of our human faculties.

4 Culture and identity

GAR'S memories (and hence the consciousness of the audience) extend over the 25 years following the introduction, by Eamon de Valera, of the 1937 constitution. In the first episode of the play we learn that Maire and S.B. were married on 1 January 1937. De Valera's constitution was enacted by referendum on 1 July 1937. The constitution gave a central place to the family in the life of the nation.

The articles dealing with family rights and social policy were derived from the papal encyclicals of Pope Pius XI and reflected the contemporary social teaching of the Catholic Church. There is a fine irony in *Philadelphia, Here I Come!* in the implicit contrast between the constitutional emphasis on the family and the importance of marriage, and the failure of these institutions to provide any kind of emotional and personal fulfilment for the characters in the drama. Indeed, the play as a whole registers a disillusionment with the inertia and stupefaction of public and private life, and the failure of both the church and state to provide moral and social leadership. This failure is evident in the play's portrayal of priest and politician.

Doogan is the local politician. He is a graduate in law. In his ambitions for his daughter he betrays a determination to maintain the strong class differentiation that operates in the community. Kate will marry a university graduate, whose father was a college friend of the Senator. From Doogan's point of view, this marriage will preserve the homogeneity of the middle classes. Doogan's brief part in the drama casts doubts on the kind of political leadership that can be given by someone as anxious as he to preserve the existing social hierarchies.

Equally uninspiring is the figure of Canon Mick O'Byrne. Both as parish priest and as manager of the national school, he occupies a position of immense influence in the community. As a spiritual leader, he has the opportunity to give hope to his parishioners by bringing to them the message of Christianity. However, as we encounter him in the play, he has settled into a life of ease and routine. He has no words of support, consolation or wisdom for S.B., on the eve of Gar's departure. He and the

Senator represent 'the rulers — the establishment — who pretend to believe in a traditional social structure that is Christian in origin, that is now seen to be false, but which they still pretend to believe in in order to give them the authority they require.' (Brian Friel)

The political and spiritual inertia of the community of Ballybeg make it difficult for Gar to belong. This difficulty is compounded by the fragmented culture that he inherits. This fragmented inheritance is revealed most clearly in the variety of voices through which Gar speaks. In the opening episode, he rehearses Burke's lines from his *Reflections on the Revolution in France*. It is interesting that he should recite these lines. Burke represented an Anglo-Irish and royalist tradition. His view of the French monarchy, and of Marie Antoinette, was a fiction created with the intention of discrediting the revolution and its radical politics. Burke's celebration of an idealised past calls into question an imperfect present. Gar, too, frequently looks back to an idealised and fictional past, which somehow calls into question his unhappy present. His 'memories' of his mother's spirit and vitality stand as an accusation against his father's awkward and cumbersome personality.

Having spoken the lines from Burke, Gar then assumes a new identity and speaks in the voice of an American cowboy. In the Hollywood version of the American myth, the cowboy opened up the American frontier, and was instrumental in shaping the future of the emerging nation. The cowboy owed nothing to the tradition and culture of Europe. He was not interested in the past, or in his ties with the 'old world'. It is altogether appropriate that Gar should speak in this voice before his departure to Philadelphia.

The switch from one voice to the other dramatises the central conflict in the play — a conflict between Gar's emotional loyalty to the past and his desire to create an identity for himself that is free of the past. Gar, however, is not merely caught between the past and the future, between an Anglo-Irish and an American culture. The Mendelssohn record and its importance for Gar is indicative of a European 'high' culture, a culture that Gar has partly assimilated. The Mendelssohn record speaks to and for Gar:

> Listen! Listen! Listen! D'you hear it? D'you know what the
> music says? *(To S.B.)* It says that once upon a time a boy and
> his father sat in a blue boat on a lake on an afternoon in May,
> and on that afternoon a great beauty happened, a beauty that
> has haunted the boy ever since . . . (p. 98)

But the music is mere 'noise' to the Canon, and means nothing to S.B. The Mendelssohn record symbolises the distance between father and son. Gar aspires to a wider culture than the provincial, Catholic one of his father. However, the voices of a Catholic, Gaelic Ireland are equally present in his imagination. In remembering his mother, Gar recites the prayers for the dead; as he is eejiting about he lilts some ceilidhe music; as he thinks of Kate Doogan he sings 'She Moved through the Fair'.

The variety of voices through which Gar speaks expresses his confused cultural inheritance, an inheritance that embraces an Anglo-Irish and popular American tradition, in addition to indigenous folk and European Art traditions. Yet for all these voices, he cannot find his own language, nor speak in a voice that is truly his. His restlessness and failure to achieve a sustained sense of self may be attributed, in part, to the multiplicity of languages available to him. When Gar recreates in his imagination a happier past, he finds an authentic form of self-expression. This voice, however, fails to find public expression. If, as Madge suggests, Gar will become as silent as S.B., then he will never find a way of communicating the truth and substance of his inner self.

The Characters

GAR O'DONNELL

PUBLIC AND PRIVATE — TWO VIEWS OF THE ONE MAN

The most striking dramatic technique in the play is the use of two actors to portray Gar's character. One represents the public side of his character, the aspect which is considerate, sensitive and self-effacing. The other depicts his private self, 'a palpable alter-ego', that part of his personality which is rebellious, comical and arrogant. Friel uses the technique to present a wide range of feelings, thoughts and emotions in his central character. It would not be possible to portray the personae adopted by Private in a conventional stage character without giving the impression of a fractured, even schizophrenic, personality. Through this technique, we have a privileged view of Gar's interior life. Gar Private can express what is normally suppressed and thus highlight the frustrations and aggressions of his inner self. From a theatrical point of view, the revelation of two sides of Gar's character allows Friel to add a sense of energy and vitality to the play, to extend the tone and variety of language, and to exploit the comic possibilities of the dual personality.

The public side of Gar's character is sullen, reticent, almost monosyllabic in speech; his talk is perfunctory, he is unexpressive and, in the interview with Senator Doogan, tongue-tied and idiotic. This contrasts sharply with Private's witty, eloquent, imaginative and colourful performance. Private is loquacious, brilliant, intelligent, shrewd and aware of his own failings as much as he is aware of the inadequacies of those around him. As Seamus Deane points out in his *Introduction to the Selected Plays of Brian Friel:* 'Although *Philadelphia* was a remarkable play, prefiguring some of the later work in its preoccupations, it was a virtuoso performance of the kind of Irish eloquence which had come to be expected from Irish playwrights in particular. It was "fine writing". The horrifying stupefied condition of the Irish social and political world which it also revealed was treated almost as a foil to that brilliant chat of Gar O'Donnell.' The 'brilliant chat' of Gar O'Donnell is more correctly the 'brilliant chat' of Gar Private — 'the unseen man, the man within, the conscience, the alter-ego, the secret thoughts, the id' (p. 11). The effect of his eloquence is to highlight the impoverishment and narrowness of the world around him.

The technique of dual personality reflects a duality which runs right through the play. Duality characterises Gar's relationship with his father, for instance. On the one hand he is mocking and abusive; on the other he longs for some sign or gesture of love. There is a constant conflict in his personality: a conflict between the desire to be free and his need to be affirmed by those closest to him. Gar does not address his problems directly: when he does communicate his unhappiness and frustration, it is directed towards the wrong person. He does not communicate with his father; he fails to make any coherent response to Senator Doogan; he doesn't ask Boyle any questions about Maire; and he fails to converse with the Canon.

 THE ADOLESCENT GAR

Outwardly, Gar is self-conscious, tongue-tied and often sullen; inwardly, there is a rush of energy and emotions, bantering talk and fantasies. His failure to find a consistent identity is marked by changing moods and the extraordinary variety of his fantasies. We may ask is Gar going to be a footballer, a pilot, an orchestra conductor, a hotel manager, a ladies man, a cowboy or a violinist? He speaks in different voices and accents; at various times, he wanders from poetic clichés to romanticism and then to bawdy and silly talk. The range of emotions reflected in these fantasies is remarkable: it oscillates between anger, frustration, exuberance and abandon. His mind is still adolescent and needs real life experience to bring it to maturity.

All of Gar's relationships, particularly his relationships with women, reflect his lack of experience and hence his immaturity. His love for Kate is an extension of his adolescent fantasies. She is the woman who will satisfy his sexual desires:

> Public: Kate — Kathy — I'm mad about you: I'll never last
> till Easter! I'll — I'll — I'll bloody-well burst! (p. 28)

and later in the scene:

Public: *(Grabs her again):* God, Kate, I can't even wait till
          Christmas!
Kate: Shhhhh.
Public: But I can't. We'll have to get married sooner — next
          month — next week — (p. 30)

However, when Gar is confronted with the reality of asking Senator
Doogan for Kate's hand in marriage, his private eloquence becomes Public's
reticence — he becomes the clown and his immaturity is revealed.

We learn more of Gar's attitude to women in his fantasies. He refers to
himself as an 'aul rooster' and imagines himself being accompanied by
gorgeous American women. He has assimilated many of the attitudes of 'the
boys', but whereas their fantastic exploits are centered around the women of
Ballybeg or the occasional women visitors, Gar has broadened the scope of his
fantasies. In his world, women are presented as exotic and seductive creatures:

> Karin — that's her name — no — ah — ah — Tamara —
> *(caressing the word).* Tamara — grand-daughter of an exiled
> Russian prince, and you'll be consumed by a magnificent
> passion; and this night you'll invite her to dinner in your
> penthouse, and you'll be dressed in a deep blue velvet jacket,
> and the candles will discover magic fairy lights in her hair,
> and you'll say to her, 'Tamara,' and she'll incline her face
> towards you, and close her eyes, and whisper — (p. 88)

In contrast to the glamorised women of Gar's fantasies, the 'real'
women in his life are very prosaic: Madge is referred to as 'aul fluke-feet'
(p. 54) and Lizzy is smothering and drunken. Madge is, in effect, his mother
— he is at ease with her, he confides in her, he loves her and he is jealous of
her love for her own relatives. She is restrained in her affection towards
him: her love is displayed in secretive acts of kindness (inviting 'the boys' to
visit Gar and hiding two pounds in Gar's coat-pocket). Gar accepts Madge's
affection and usually takes it for granted. Lizzy, on the other hand, displays
her emotions overtly. Her love is expressed by touching and embracing. Her
offer to be Gar's 'mother' terrifies him because it is so blatant and
smothering. In reality, he recoils from overt displays of affection, though he
fantasises about love. Throughout the play he yearns for affection but he
cannot countenance it when it is offered to him. ('Not yet! Don't touch me
yet!' p. 64). Lizzy's remark that the O'Donnells are 'kinda cold' is seen to be
true in Gar's case: he is deeply disturbed by Master Boyle's embrace,

terrified by Lizzy's motherly hug, and emotionally moved by Ned's awkward gesture of affection. The loss of his mother, his father's inability to compensate emotionally for this loss, and the habitual reticence of the Irish community with regard to matters of love, explain Gar's awkwardness and embarrassment in the face of emotional expression, and the adolescent nature of his real and imaginary relationships with women.

GAR AND THE AMERICAN DREAM

For Gar, Philadelphia opens up a vast array of possibilities, and his fantasies are nothing if not ambitious. He might become Chairman of General Motors, the President of the biggest chain of hotels in the world, a famous orchestra conductor or a Hollywood star. In Gar's case, America is the land of 'second' opportunity. Having failed at UCD, the possibilities for his future were extremely limited. He returned to Ballybeg and to his father's store where the only opportunity for self-enterprise amounts to secretly selling a few eggs to increase his wages by a mere pittance. In his dreams, America is glamorous and materially rewarding. But Gar can also view these dreams sardonically:

> Public: You will begin at the Emperor Hotel on Monday 23rd, which is about twenty minutes away.
> Private: Monsieur, madam.
> Public: Con says it is a fine place for to work in and the owner is Mr Patrick Palinakis, who is half-Irish —
> Private: Patrick.
> Public: — and half-Greek.
> Private: Palinakis.
> Public: His grandfather came from County Mayo.
> Private: By the hokey! The Greek from Belmullet!
> Public: We know you will like it here and work hard.
> Private: *(rapidly):* Monsieur — madam — monsieur — madam — monsieur — madam — (pp. 55-6)

Master Boyle advised Gar to be '100 per cent American', to forget about the past and to cut his ties with Ballybeg. But Gar refuses to do so: he collects 'memories and images and impressions' which will act as a buffer to that 'vast, restless place that doesn't give a curse about the past'.

The occasion of Kate's visit gives a public airing to Gar's fantasies and ambitions for the future, but it also reveals his lack of conviction in these ambitions:

> Public: I'll probably go to night-school as well — you know,
> at night —
> Private: Brilliant.
> Public: — do law or medicine or something —
> Private: Like hell! First Arts stumped you! (pp. 79-80)

Inwardly, Gar fears for the future. He has no confidence in his ability and, even as he speaks, his inner mind is doubting the veracity of his words.

As Gar delivers a scathing invective against Ballybeg and its inhabitants, his voice gets louder and louder. It is almost as if he is trying to convince himself that the reasons for going are valid. When Kate leaves he buries his face in his hands and, with trembling fingers, lights a cigarette and takes a drink. Kate's words echo in his ears '— good-bye, Gar, it isn't as bad as that — good-bye, Gar, it isn't as bad as that — good-bye, Gar, it isn't as bad as that —' (p. 83). Ballybeg is not such a grim place: Gar fails to convince himself that he hates the place — instead, the memories of Ballybeg and its inhabitants drown out his attempted whistling of his song *Philadelphia, Here I Come!*

GAR'S ATTITUDE TO BALLYBEG

As the moment of his departure draws near, Gar questions and analyses his relationship to Ballybeg. This relationship cannot be divorced from his attitude to the inhabitants of Ballybeg, and to his father in particular. He is embarrassed by the nature of his father's business. The first indication of this occurs in his fantasy interview for the job in the hotel:

> Private: Yeah. You mentioned that your father was a
> businessman. What's his line?
> Public: Well, Sir, he has — what you would call — his
> finger in many pies — retail mostly — general dry
> goods — assorted patent drugs — hardware — ah
> — ah — dehydrated fish — men's king-size hose —
> snuffs from the exotic East . . . of Donegal — a
> confection for gourmets, known as Peggy's Leg —
> weedkiller — (p. 23)

Again, he is disparaging of his father's shop when he recalls his conversation with Kate:

> Private: Cripes, you make me laugh! You bloody-well make
> me die laughing. You were going to 'develop' the
> hardware lines and she was going to take charge of

the 'drapery'! The drapery! The fishy socks and the
shoebox of cotton spools and rusted needles! (p. 28)

In his fantasy, Gar puts a gloss on the shop's affairs when 'speaking' to
an 'American'. There is a resentment here, too, that so much of his life is
bound up with mundane matters: gutting and salting fish, stocking coils of
barbed-wire and fencing-posts, ordering plug tobacco and buying tin cans
from the tinkers. By American standards, the hardware store is a remnant
from a past civilisation: the advent of cookers and ranges ended the demand
for tin cans; S.B. and his store have not moved with the times.

Gar is genuinely frustrated by S.B.'s preoccupation with the affairs of
the shop, yet in order to communicate with his father, he must speak S.B.'s
language. Gar recognises that 'It's the silence that's the enemy' between
them and he struggles to make contact with his father at any cost.

The name Ballybeg is itself an indication of a closed parochial society.
Ballybeg — Baile Beag — Small Town — is associated with narrow horizons
and limited possibilities. By contrast, we discover that Gar's mother came
from a place called Bailtefree. She typified a young and free spirit. But in
Gar's mind, she was crushed by the oppressiveness of life in Ballybeg: 'And
sometimes in that first year, when she was pregnant with you, laddybuck,
the other young girls from Bailtefree would call in here to dress up on their
way to a dance, Madge says, and her face would light up too, Madge says . . .
And he must have known, old Screwballs, he must have known, Madge says,
for many a night he must have heard her crying herself to sleep. . . .' (p. 25).

Senator Doogan typifies the attitudes of a small town politician. His
main concern is to preserve the existing social structures. His interview
with Gar reveals his deep-rooted class consciousness. Gar lacks the personal
resources to overcome the class barriers which preclude him from marrying
the Senator's daughter. Gar's attitude to Ballybeg is closely linked with his
failure to win Kate. He needs to get away in order to come to terms with his
disappointment in love and his humiliation at the hands of the Senator. In
his final meeting with Kate, he fantasises a triumphant return to Ballybeg.
He will prove the Senator wrong:

> Public: I'll come home when I make my first million, driving a
> Cadillac and smoking cigars and taking movie-films.
>
> Kate: I hope you're very happy there and that life will be
> good to you.
>
> Public: *(slightly louder)* I'll make sure life's good to me from
> now on. (p. 80)

The strongest expression of Gar's frustration with Ballybeg and its inhabitants can be summed up in his vehement outburst to Kate:

> If I had to spend another week in Ballybeg, I'd go off my bloody head! This place would drive anybody crazy! Look around you, for God's sake! Look at Master Boyle! Look at my father! Look at the Canon! Look at the boys! Asylum cases, the whole bloody lot of them! (p. 80)

Ballybeg is seen by Gar as a place of failure: the alcoholic Boyle is 'nothing but a drunken aul schoolmaster — a conceited, arrogant wash-out!' (p. 47); S.B. fails to communicate with his son; the Canon fails to translate Gar's predicament into Christian terms; and 'the boys' are trapped in their environment of sexual frustration where their main occupation is hanging around the gable end of the hotel watching, rather than participating in, life. Gar has 'stuck around this hole far too long . . . it's a bloody quagmire, a backwater, a dead-end!' (p. 81)

However, Gar has not secured a satisfactory position or established a consistent identity for himself in Ballybeg. He is pulled towards the future, yet drawn back towards a sentimental view of the past. In many ways, Gar is an outsider, frustrated by the inhabitants of his hometown, and unable to assert an authentic sense of self. His attitude to Ballybeg is thus ambivalent. On the one hand, he claims to hate the place 'and every stone, and every rock, and every piece of heather around it!' On the other hand he stores up memories of the place:

> 'there *was* fun and there *was* laughing — foolish, silly fun and foolish, silly laughing; but what it was all about you can't remember, can you? Just the memory of it — that's all you have now — just the memory; and even now, even so soon, it is being distilled of all its coarseness; and what's left is going to be precious, precious gold . . .' (pp. 78-9)

Gar O'Donnell is an intriguing and complex character. Yet he is not a tragic hero in the classical sense. Basically, he is a young man in the throes of making the transition from adolescence to manhood. His varying moods, his frantic energy, his coarse and bawdy humour, his sentimentality and juvenile romanticism make him a sympathetic character and one with whom we can identify. We smile at his dilemma, we marvel at his ingenuity, we relish his virtuosity, we laugh at his outrageous humour and we may even shed a tear at his homesickness, but we recognise that his situation is not altogether tragic or extraordinary.

S.B. O'DONNELL

GAR'S most powerful and ambiguous feelings are directed towards his father S.B. O'Donnell. S.B. is described in the stage directions as 'a responsible, respectable citizen' (p. 21). He owns a general shop and is one of the Catholic 'petite bourgeoisie', a class mocked by Yeats in his poem *September 1913*.

His speech is primarily unexpressive and perfunctory (a characteristic he shares with his son). His life is governed by routine and the repetition of well-established custom. His every word is predictable, and his routine has acquired the status of unalterable fact. When Gar offers him a second cup of tea, his response is one of impatience and irritability: 'Sure you know I never take a second cup' (p. 41).

In his conversations with the Canon, Boyle and Gar, S.B. is detached, and maintains an awkward formal tone. He is thus infuriatingly remote from Gar. Despite the wishes and best efforts of Madge that he break the silence between himself and Gar, he cannot do so. He is trapped within a narrow repertoire of responses, and lacks the means to articulate his innermost thoughts and feelings. When Gar and he sit down to tea, the talk is of barbed wire and rats, the shop and the weather. For most of the play, we doubt whether S.B. possesses an interior life at all. The first sign of upset or agitation that we detect in him occurs when he 'reads' a paper that is upside down. He is thinking of Gar and looks wistfully to his son's room and sighs. Characteristically, no words are spoken. For her part, Madge is certain that his silence does not imply a lack of feeling:

> Madge: And another thing: just because he doesn't say much doesn't mean that he hasn't feelings like the rest of us.
>
> Public: Say much? He's said nothing!
>
> Madge: He said nothing either when your mother died. It must have been near daybreak when he got to sleep last night. I could hear his bed creaking. (p. 20)

Madge's words are of little consolation to a son seeking a sign or a token of his father's love, and S.B. is clearly incapable of giving public expression to his private feelings.

S.B. disapproves of Boyle and is 'barely courteous' to him. He addresses him as 'Master', but this formality is, more likely than not, a refusal of friendship arising from Boyle's conflict with the Canon, his rivalry for Maire, and his friendship with Gar.

. . . THE WORDS THAT ARE NOT SAID

It is in the final scene of the play that we obtain a real insight into S.B.'s character. Clearly he is upset at the prospect of Gar's impending departure, but equally he is embarrassed to be discovered up and about in the middle of the night. In the unusual circumstances one might expect S.B. to be freer in his expression, but his remarks remain guarded and cautious. Tentatively, he broachs the subject of Gar's departure: 'You're getting the mail-van to Strabane?' With painful self-consciousness, he offers Gar advice on where to sit on the plane, but immediately disowns his remarks, crediting the Canon with their authorship. Clearly, he lacks the personal and emotional resources to communicate with his son. The failure is both his and the community's in general. It is a failure to develop a language capable of expressing personal feelings without embarrassment or self-consciousness. Gar, sensing something of S.B.'s mood, directs the conversation towards his most cherished memory of their relationship — the day on Lough na Cloc Cor. As he does so, his voice quickens with excitement and anticipation. But S.B. cannot make the imaginative or emotional leap required to recognise the significance of his son's words. Instead of offering his love for Gar, he clumsily searches out the 'truth' of Gar's memories, and the moment is lost.

Ironically, when Gar retires, S.B. begins to give voice to his feelings for his son in the 'sailor-suit' reverie. Tragically for S.B. and Gar, the words are addressed to Madge. To her he acknowledges his failure and disappointment:

> S.B.:   . . . Maybe, Madge, maybe it's because I could have
>   been his grandfather, eh?
> Madge: I don't know.
> S.B.:   I was too old for her, Madge, eh? (pp. 107-8)

The tone is filled with regret and fatalism, as if S.B. feels himself confronted by an unalterable and debilitating reality. Suddenly S.B. is revealed as weak, vulnerable and helpless. He looks to Madge for reassurance and support. Madge, much taken for granted, is ever present as nurse and comforter. Her presence is one of the few compensations in a life that has been unfulfilled and disappointing: he was too old for his young wife; he was too old for his son. More than anyone else, Madge understands S.B.'s disappointment, recognises and is loyal to his essential decency, and caters for his helplessness.

MADGE

THE opening line of the play is delivered by Madge and 'Madge Going to Bed On My Last Night at Home' is Gar's final image. At first glance she may appear to be only a functionary character, a domestic servant who brings in the tea, caters for the needs of the O'Donnells and their visitors, assists in the running of the shop and makes passing comments about the other characters. But her role is much more important than that.

THE VOICE OF REALITY

Madge is a realist and in contrast to Gar, S.B., Boyle, the Canon and 'the boys', who are all incapable of decisive action, she manages the household and quietly gets her work done. When Gar's mother died, she took upon herself the job of rearing the young boy and even though he is now a young man of twenty-five, she still caters for his domestic needs and reprimands him in a motherly way: 'And there's your shirts and your winter vests and your heavy socks. And you'll need to air them shirts before you — Don't put them smelly hands on them! (p. 19).

In contrast to Gar, who reveals his inner thoughts through the 'silent' voice of Private, Madge is not afraid to say what she really thinks about the other characters. Boyle, making his hasty exit to the pub, bumps into Madge at the scullery door and she spares him no embarrassment with her tongue-

lashing: 'Lord, the speed of him! His tongue out for a drink!' (p. 47). She is
equally forthright towards the Canon: 'She says I wait till the rosary's over
and the kettle's on . . .' (p. 91) and although he attempts to sneer at her
implied slight at his lack of observance of the rosary ritual, the fact that he
repeats the remark many times during the draughts game, shows that her
observation carries a ring of truth to it. Madge's remark emphasises Gar's
assertion that the Canon is a failure in Christian terms. The Canon is
content to be comfortable in his position as spiritual leader of his
community without making any sacrifice or addressing the problems of his
parishioners. Through Madge and Gar, Friel highlights the fact that a life of
ease is incompatible with a life of religion. Inwardly, Gar condemns the
Canon but Madge voices her feelings without hesitation.

Madge's sharp and humorous baiting of self-delusion is clearly seen in
her references to 'the boys'. She recognises that 'the boys' are not boys at all:
'How many of them are getting the pension now?' (p. 66) is an obvious
reference to their advanced years. She also has doubts about the value of
their friendship and loyalty to Gar, and when they finally come to visit him
she comments coldly on the level of noise that they are making: 'Just thought
I heard somebody whispering.' (p. 69). When Ned betrays his lack of social
decorum by belching, she sarcastically reprimands him: 'Mister Sweeney, too;
gentlemanly as ever.' (p. 69). She does not reveal, however, that it was she
who invited 'the boys' to come to the O'Donnell household: her discreet
invitation is an indication of her concern for Gar. She did not wish him to be
hurt or humiliated by the absence of his friends on his last night in Ballybeg.

Madge is unwilling to collaborate with other people's illusions. She is a
character who speaks the truth. She lacks the status of the 'titled' people in
the play but, unlike the Senator, the Master, the Canon or the County
Councillor, she has no illusions about her social position. She accepts the
world as she finds it and she is not afraid to express her true feelings about
other people. She is the voice of realism and truth in the play.

MADGE AS INTERMEDIARY

Throughout the play, Madge acts as an intermediary between S.B. and Gar.
At first, she believes that S.B. will make a gesture of affection towards Gar.
But as the play unfolds she realises that S.B. is not going to say or do
anything to demonstrate his sense of loss at his son's leaving, and the irony is

that it is Madge who places two pounds in Gar's coat-pocket in the final scene. Madge observes the growing frustration in Gar due to his father's silence, yet she is careful not to condemn S.B. Rather, she tries to explain the lack of communication by telling Gar that 'He *(S.B.)* said nothing either when your mother died. It must have been near daybreak when he got to sleep last night. I could hear his bed creaking.' (p. 20). Here Madge indicates that S.B. is upset about his son's departure and that his inability to state these feelings in words 'doesn't mean that he hasn't feelings like the rest of us ' (p. 20). Her most direct intervention in trying to heal the communication gap between father and son occurs during the tea-time scene. On two occasions she comments on the absence of conversation between the two. Giving S.B. a hard look, in a voice heavy with irony she says: 'The chatting in this place would deafen a body. Won't the house be quiet soon enough — long enough?' (p. 41) and again: 'A body couldn't get a word in edgeways with you two!' (p. 42)

Madge's efforts to get S.B. and Gar to communicate are in vain. The irony of the play is that S.B. and Gar have no difficulty in communicating their feelings to Madge; S.B.'s moving description of Gar as a boy dressed in a sailor-suit, father and son 'as happy as larks', would have proven to Gar that his father did have precious memories of the past, but S.B. talks to Madge, not to Gar, about this memory. Up to the final episode Madge still hopes that S.B. and Gar will talk to each other. When she returns from her visit to the Mulhern house she asks Gar: 'Were you and the boss chatting there?' (p. 109), but Gar immediately changes the subject. Madge too, has her own private disappointment — the fact that her niece's baby was not named after her. But she says nothing about this to Gar although she shares her disappointment with S.B. All the characters have their private disappointments, but they communicate their feelings to the wrong people. In her role as intermediary between S.B. and Gar, Madge has to bear the sorrow of the son's exile coupled with the frustration of the father's inability to communicate his true feelings to the one who matters most.

MADGE'S WORLDLY WISDOM

Madge can cope with the reality of events and her worldly wisdom puts Gar's conflict about leaving home into proper perspective. She knows that his grief will be short-lived: 'Tomorrow'll be sore on him *(Gar):* his heart'll break tomorrow, and all next week, and the week after maybe . . .' Through her voice, the voice of age and wisdom, we recognise that Gar's quandary is part of the nature of life. Her final monologue, accompanied by her gesture of 'vague Benediction', interprets the conflict of Gar's exile and transposes it from the level of the extraordinary, to the more ordinary level of the continuum of life. Madge recognises that Gar belongs to 'a new race — a new world'; S.B. has gone through the turmoil of his life — he has passed the phase of 'leppin', and eejitin' about and actin' the clown'; Gar in his turn, will also go through the natural process of growing up and 'he'll turn out just the same'. She realises that what Gar is going through is 'simply continuance, life repeating itself and surviving'.

Madge, the simple housekeeper, speaks with the wisdom of age and common sense. She is the yardstick by which the audience can judge and evaluate the fantasy, romanticism, buffoonery and role-playing of the central character. Her earthy philosophy of life counterpoints the loquacious banter of Gar and provides a dimension of realism and ordinariness which gives extra depth and meaning to Philadelphia. As such she plays a significant part in the unfolding of the drama.

KATE DOOGAN

KATE Doogan is the object of Gar's love, desire and frustration. His attitude to her is ambivalent, and, in many respects unfair. She is accused of a snobbishness that more correctly belongs to her father. After the debacle of the interview with the Senator, she is made the scapegoat for Gar's failure and inadequacy.

As soon as we hear her first lines in the play, we recognise Kate's pragmatism. She is aware (as with the women in O'Casey) of the necessities of life and love. She forces Gar to consider their financial situation, and its bearing on their future. In contrast to his romantic and juvenile notions, she ponders the meagreness of his wages. Kate realises that his lack of income will prove an obstacle in obtaining the consent of her parents to their marriage. Consequently, she rehearses Gar in a fiction that will be acceptable to her father: 'You have £20 a week and £5,000 in the bank and your father's about to retire' (p. 31). What she has not anticipated is her father's social pretensions.

Gar is irritated by her insistence that he address the matter of his earnings. In a fit of petulance, he reveals the secret of the 'egg-money', his private source of income. At that moment Gar is the immature Romeo to Kate's strong-willed Juliet. Kate acts boldly and with authority in bringing Gar before her father. She is bound by the conventions and strictures of a patriarchal society, but she is spirited enough to wish to subvert these conventions. However, to reject the future mapped out for her by her father, Kate must look to Gar as her champion. As they enter the Doogan household, she kisses Gar passionately, strengthening his resolve. But Gar lacks the courage and poise to carry off her audacious plan. He fails Kate and himself, and she is married to Francis King, as her parents had desired.

We are told little of the marriage, but it is surely significant that the story of S.B.'s and Maire's wedding is recounted to Gar on the day of Kate's wedding. The manner in which the two marriages are associated and juxtaposed may suggest that the marriages are alike. In each case the reason for marrying was social, and there are strong indications that neither woman was in love with the man she married. When Kate comes to say farewell to Gar, she makes one remark which supports this reading of her marriage. In response to Gar's enquiring for Dr King, she replies, 'I hear no complaints' (p. 80). It is a severe, even pained, reply. Her visit demonstrates a continued affection for Gar, though she is careful to style herself an 'old friend'. However much a source of disappointment her marriage may be, it is for better or worse. Her marriage and its vows are absolute. It is a further indication of her understanding of the social realities, and contrasts sharply with both Gar and Boyle's hankering for the past, and its unfulfilled hopes.

Kate speaks clearly and perceptively of how Gar's departure will affect S.B. To this, and to her other remarks, Gar responds in an aggressive manner, hiding his love in a loud and ungracious tone. As she leaves to return to a husband who will 'be wondering what's keeping' her, Gar's tone becomes coarse and gross. For the second time in the play he fails Kate and himself.

Kate possesses many of the qualities evident in the women of O'Casey's and Synge's plays. She is practical and honest; she speaks directly and with sincerity; she is dignified and resigned in disappointment. Kate is conscious of the social realities that shape and govern her life, and, unable to subvert them, she accepts the limitations they impose. Ultimately, she is forced to live within a narrow range of possibilities, and accepts her lot in a manner that is both restrained and dignified.

SENATOR DOOGAN

SENATOR Doogan is the voice of political authority in the play. His is a voice that is male, confident and composed, the voice of middle-class Ireland. It is condescending, if kindly.

Doogan is well practised in the art of persuasion. He anticipates the object of Gar's visit to his home, and engages him in a battle of wit and eloquence before Gar realises what is happening. Gar is no match for his adversary, scarcely recognising him as such in the course of their interview. By addressing him as 'Gareth', Doogan appears to include Gar among his class. If Gar is to respond in kind, he must affect an air of easy complacency. Before Gar has any chance to achieve this, Doogan introduces Francis King into the conversation. This is casually done ('You've met Francis King, haven't you, Gareth?' p. 32). But the effect is calculated. Gar falters ('Yes — yes —') and Doogan immediately yokes together King and Kate, misrepresenting 'Kate's hopes', sharing the news as if with an intimate. Gar is now demoralised and fails to notice the transfer from Kate's hopes to her father's hopes ('her mother and I . . . let's say we're living in hope' p. 32).

Gar's discomfort is increased by the talk of 'graduate', 'university' and 'class fellows at school'. This certainly excludes Gar from the intimate circle of Doogan's world. The social distance between them is further emphasised when Doogan switches the conversation from his old college friend to enquire for S.B. Gar is left to conclude how little the son of a grocer has in common with the family of a Senator and law graduate. At this point Gar makes an undignified retreat. As he does so, Doogan attempts to soften the humiliation, but there is an evident, if unwitting, hypocrisy in his claim that Kate's happiness is his only concern. The audience may be justified in believing that the preservation of his social class and the perpetuation of class structure were his real concerns.

Through the character of Doogan, Brian Friel hints at the political inertia of the country in the decades following the war. Doogan's concern is with cultivating the right social connections, and maintaining the homogeneity of his class. It is hardly an attitude or outlook that will lead to an enlightened political vision. In the persons of the Canon, Boyle and Doogan, we recognise the failure of religion, literature and politics to serve the needs of the community. The Canon has chosen the option of non-involvement; Boyle's writing is a wholly private affair; Doogan's politics, we may assume, are those of self-aggrandisement.

MASTER BOYLE

A S the local 'master', Boyle occupies an influential position in Ballybeg. Traditionally, scholarship and poetry have commanded widespread respect in Irish society. Boyle aspires to be both scholar and poet, and adopts the defiant and rebellious posture of the artist. He is, in the tradition of the poet, in conflict with the clergy. This conflict has taken on a legendary aspect in which appearance matters more than reality: he confides to Gar that he feels 'a particular attachment' for the Canon, despite their widely publicised disagreements.

To Gar, Boyle appears 'arrogant and pathetic'. He speaks the language of freedom, but is trapped in the past, and is unable to break free of the place most associated with the past — Ballybeg. Even as he takes leave of Gar (en route to the pub) the past is invoked. He recalls the Gallagher girls, reciting a litany of their names. The litany begins and ends with 'Maire', Gar's mother. Gar believes that Boyle's disappointment in love drove him to drink. This romantic notion redeems Boyle in Gar's eyes, for Gar too, of course, has suffered the disappointment of an unfulfilled love.

Boyle, as Gar suggests, is arrogant, yet he is also unsure of his own talent and worth. His lack of confidence leads to many sly assertions of his intellectual superiority over his former pupil. It also leads to Boyle publishing his work privately. The private publication of one's own work avoids the possibility of rejection and failure, and Boyle fears failure to the point of telling transparent lies concerning his 'success'. Hence the story of an offer from a university in Boston to head its education department. But neither his vanity nor his self-preoccupation prevent the audience from recognising an idealism grown bitter and a life marked by loneliness.

Boyle is the only person to tell Gar that he is doing the right thing in leaving Ballybeg. In this, he transfers his own feelings and disappointments onto Gar. Gar is to be '100 per cent American' . He is to 'Forget Ballybeg and Ireland'. In short, he is to escape the nightmare of the past, which has made Boyle's life a lonely and embittered one. The Master's loneliness is especially evident in his memories of Gar. In a life that had known happiness and satisfaction, the events which he recalls would not have been significant:

> Do you remember the Christmas you sent me the packet of
> cigarettes? And the day you brought me a pot of jam to the
> digs? It was you, wasn't it? (p. 45)

Gar is sure of Boyle; he is unsure of S.B. Gar's feelings for S.B. are tainted by two accusations or doubts that he harbours against him, two questions that Gar wishes resolved: did S.B. really love Maire?; does S.B. really love Gar? S.B., for his part, is not friendly towards Boyle. He is formal in his address, conferring on him the title 'Master'. Whether this is an indication of his respect for Boyle's learning and social status or a means of denying him any show of friendship, is not clear. There are enough reasons for S.B.'s hostility. Boyle had been a rival for Maire's affection, and is now a rival for Gar's. He is in conflict with the Canon, a nightly visitor to S.B.'s home.

Madge is dismissive of Boyle and scornful of his need for drink. She is unwilling to give Gar any support in his estimation of Boyle, telling him that his mother 'married the better man by far' (p. 94). In her loyalty to S.B., Madge displays a censorious and intolerant attitude to Boyle. Self-pity, of course, is a luxury that Madge cannot afford, though her life has not been a model of happiness and completion.

Boyle is weak-willed. He possesses a knowledge of what he would like to be, but lacks the energy or courage to achieve it. His farewell to Gar is tinged with self-interest and a strong ambition to prove himself — he seizes the opportunity to ask Gar to send him the names of some magazines that publish the occasional poem. His need for drink robs him of his dignity and he seeks a handout (not a loan) from Gar. His failings, then, are obvious. He is, in Private's words, 'nothing but a drunken aul schoolmaster — a conceited, arrogant wash-out!' However, there is more to Boyle than his weakness, and Gar's relationship to him is more than that of a former pupil to his old schoolmaster. Boyle loved Gar's mother, and the failure of his life bears witness in a strange way to the strength of his love for her. His love for Maire is the past that he cannot escape. Moreover, Boyle expresses a genuine affection and regard for Gar: the book of poetry symbolises it, his words speak it, his embrace acts it.

CANON MICK O'BYRNE

'WHEN he (the modern dramatist) says that governments are bungling, he's right. When he says the church is fumbling, he's right'. (*The Theatre of Hope and Despair)*

Canon Mick O'Byrne is the representative of ecclesiastical authority in the play. Both as parish priest and manager of the national school, he wields considerable power in the community of Ballybeg. We learn something of him through the other characters in the play. Boyle informs us that he and the Canon are in conflict — the Canon wishing to be rid of Boyle from the school. (Madge and S.B. appear to share the Canon's antipathy.) Gar states that the Canon is 'warm and kind and soft and sympathetic', but accuses him of failing to speak the Christian message, of preferring a life of ease to a life of real commitment. Gar accuses the Canon of silence, silence in the face of loneliness and isolation:

> because you could translate all this loneliness, this groping, this dreadful bloody buffoonery into Christian terms that will make life bearable for us all. And yet you don't say a word. Why, Canon? Why, arid Canon. Isn't this your job? — to translate? Why don't you speak, then? (p. 96)

The Canon's entrance on stage coincides with the ending of the nightly rosary in the O'Donnell household. Madge appreciates the irony of his timing. The Canon is a nightly visitor, but his talk is not the easy talk of familiarity and closeness. He and S.B. share a tone of detached formality. (S.B. refers to him consistently as 'Canon'.) His remarks on Gar's departure are routine and empty. He is content to remain in the secure world of the predictable. Gar's departure and its meaning for S.B. — the loss of his only son — demand some word of comfort or wisdom, but excite no comment other than the banal observation: 'Powerful the way time passes, too' (p. 92). This remark is echoed by S.B. later (p. 99). The meagreness of the Canon's response to a major crisis in the life of his friend forces one to acknowledge the justice of Gar's accusations. The Canon is not responding to the needs and difficulties of his parishioners — in this instance, the need for a father and son to know that each is loved by the other. It is Madge who takes upon herself the task of attempting to break the silence between S.B. and Gar.

Through the Canon, Friel expresses his dissatisfaction at the Church's failure to lead and to be in real communication with its members. The family is championed by the Church as the custodian and transmitter of traditional Catholic values. Paradoxically, the Canon offers little support to the O'Donnell family. He is accused not for what he is, or what he does, but for his failure to minister to the human needs of those amongst whom he lives.

LIZZY SWEENEY

LIZZY Sweeney is the character who comes closest to giving public expression to many of the character traits evident in Gar Private. She is loquacious, energetic and histrionic. Before we encounter her on stage, Gar makes fun of her letter to him and the social pretensions it reveals. He remembers how he could not take his eyes from her when she came to visit them the previous year. She was his mother's sister, a living image of the woman he had never known. Looking to the future in Philadelphia, he entertains misgivings about her vulgarity and smothering motherliness.

And then we meet her in mid-sentence, as it were. Her speech is essentially narrative, and she recounts her stories with a breath-taking virtuosity. She punctuates her narrative with occasional comments on the people of her stories. These asides tend towards sentimentality and Con tries to counter their effect by reminding her of where she was in the telling of her tale. Lizzy aggressively rebukes his intrusion into her performance and feigns an air of confidence and assertion. This 'confidence' is clearly demonstrated in her account of Con's first job, and the year of their departure for America. Con's minor corrections of two factual details are summarily dismissed.

Lizzy's speech contains many American expressions which appear brash and vulgar. It is as if she is forcefully identifying herself with the country of her adoption, and trying to express something of its confidence in her style of speaking. Many of her remarks show a preoccupation with money and material possessions: 'He gives us dough'; 'this guy with a big store'; 'doing big deals out there, honey, huh?'; 'We have this ground-floor apartment, see, and a car that's air-conditioned, and colour TV, and this big collection of all the Irish records you ever heard, and 15,000 bucks in Federal Bonds . . .'. In an obvious way she wishes to show how much better off she is than her relatives in Ireland. Hence her mocking remarks to Madge.

Lizzy is dismissive of Public's 'typical Irish' response, while at the same time she is possessive of her Irish identity when Ben Burton shows a surer sense of Irish affairs than she. Her simultaneous dismissal and possession of an Irish identity is characteristic of many returned exiles, whose attitude to their birthplace contains many unresolved ambiguities. She appears somewhat dismayed at S.B.'s absence. It disturbs her sense of superiority, and she questions, with some impatience, his whereabouts.

There is a further ambiguity in Lizzy's attitude to Con. Many of her remarks are implicitly disparaging: she did not marry 'a guy with a big store'; Ben Burton supported them 'until bonzo *(Con)* finally gets himself this job'; she is 'stuck with Rudolph Valentino'. In the final example, the deprecation is hardly concealed. When she compliments Ben Burton on his 'great intellect', the unstated comparison is clearly felt. It is Ben whom she kisses and to whom she pays court. However, for an Irish Catholic (and Lizzy identifies herself as such), the marriage vow is absolute. Ben Burton is a foil to her brilliance — not a threat to her marriage. Con is a foil to her wit, and a victim of her eloquence and sharp tongue. He is a willing scapegoat for her disappointments and failures.

Behind the apparent brilliance of Lizzy's performance, there lies an emptiness. As the scene develops we realise the object of her visit. She hungers for a child, and the failure to have one robs her life of completion and meaning. In speaking out of her great need, she addresses Con with obvious love, including him in her sense of loss:

> — and we spent a fortune on doctors, didn't we, Connie, but it was no good, and then I says to him (Con), 'We'll go home to Ireland', I says, 'and Maire's boy, we'll offer him everything we have —' (p. 63)

In coming to Gar she hopes to fill the void in her own life. She risks his contempt and her own dignity in the final anguished confession of her purpose. Gar's acceptance of the offer allows her to claim him as her son, but the claim is both illusory and theatrical — it is nothing less than fantasy.

CON SWEENEY

IN the stage directions Con Sweeney is referred to as 'a quiet, patient man'. As the scene unfolds, we quickly sense that he has previously heard all of what Lizzy has to say. He demonstrates a tired resignation in the face of her loquacity. Repeatedly, he 'spreads his hands in resignation'. It is his most characteristic gesture. When Lizzy's effusive narrative wanders off the point, he prompts her, keeping her to her lines: 'You were telling us a story about the morning they got married, honey, in Bailtefree chapel' (p. 61). In return, she is brusque with him to the point of rudeness. His self-effacement allows him to endure her public disregard for his every utterance.

At the moment when Lizzy's performance threatens to lapse into absolute melodrama, he utters a restraining and concerned 'Honey'. He goes on to address her as 'Elise' when her pathetic plea to Gar comes close to self-humiliation. In addressing her in this form, he restores to her a degree of dignity and self-worth. In other ways he is attentive and alert, reminding her, for example, of her gloves, as they prepare to leave.

Twice Con addresses Gar as 'son', emphasising the childlessness of his own marriage, and revealing a paternal attitude to his wife's nephew. His invitation to Gar to come to Philadelphia is undoubtedly genuine, but he is unwilling to force the issue, and speaks in moderate terms:

Con:	You'll think about what we were discussing?
Public:	I will, Uncle Con.
Con:	The job's as good as you'll get and we'd be proud to have you.
Lizzy:	Don't force him.
Con:	I'm not forcing him. I'm only telling him. (p. 60)

Con's relationship with Lizzy is an unequal one. It is he who is accommodating and attentive, while she commands the centre of the stage. His love is both suffering and loyal. Essentially, their love is unbalanced, lacking, as it is, in reciprocity and mutual regard. There is only one moment in Lizzy's talk when she includes Con as an intimate, and this deals with their failure to have a child: 'and we spent a fortune on doctors, didn't we, Connie, but it was no good . . .' (p. 63). It is a shared loss and disappointment, one that unites them and commands Con's devoted love.

BEN BURTON

THE American Ben Burton plays a small but significant part in the drama. He is the inscrutable foreigner, 'smiling into his glass'. He typifies and personifies what America has traditionally offered the emigrant Irish: a welcome, an acceptance, a chance in life, a foot up the ladder of material well-being. Lizzy recounts his kindness to them:

> He gives us this apartment. He gives us dough. He gives us three meals a day — until bonzo *(Con)* finally gets himself this job. Looks after us like we were his own skin and bone. (pp. 58-9)

In return he receives their gratitude and continual friendship. Throughout the scene he remains quiet and self-assured, in sharp contrast to the brash and loquacious Lizzy. He accepts her extravagant praises and attention with ease. When Lizzy proclaims America as 'Gawd's own country' (p. 62), his reply is a model of sense and moderation: 'It's just another place to live, Elise. Ireland — America — what's the difference?' (p. 62).

As Lizzy's anguish threatens to overcome her, he tactfully withdraws to 'get the car'. Thus he reveals an awareness of his position in the triangular relationship, notwithstanding Lizzy's flirtatious behaviour. He is a friend to them both, no more and, obviously, no less. Friel himself made some interesting comments on the character and role of Ben Burton, shortly after the play was first performed: 'I think you find that a lot in Irish marriages, there is another man floating like a satellite around the couple. A person in whom the wife confides, probably. There is nothing sinister in this and certainly nothing sexual' *(Guardian* 8 Oct. 1964).

The impression Ben Burton creates is of someone at ease with himself, an effect that throws into perspective the uncertainties and ambiguities that characterise Lizzy. His American self-assurance highlights her Irish selfconsciousness. We admire him for his constraint, generosity and tact. In Gar's words, Ben Burton is 'a right skin'; a 'Right sort'.

Dramatic Techniques

FRIEL, THE DRAMATIST

BRIAN Friel's contribution to modern drama has been considerable. Over a period of twenty years, he has produced a substantial body of work and greatly extended the range and interest of realist theatre in Ireland. He can be ranked with Samuel Beckett as the most outstanding Irish dramatist since O'Casey.

Brian Friel was born in Omagh in 1929. At the age of ten he moved to Derry, where his father obtained a teaching position in a national school. Friel was educated there and later attended Maynooth College. After College he returned to Derry and taught for several years. During this time he published his first collection of short stories, *The Saucer of Larks* (1959). In 1960 he resigned from teaching and began to work full-time on his writing. He was encouraged in this by the BBC's acceptance of two plays for radio. In 1962 he achieved his first stage success with the Abbey Theatre's production of *The Enemy Within,* a study of St. Colmcille. Two years later *Philadelphia, Here I Come!* was well received at the Dublin Theatre Festival and established an international audience for Friel's work. The play was produced on Broadway in 1966, and had a London production in the following year.

Friel's reputation was established and enhanced by a succession of plays produced throughout the 60s and 70s. These included *The Loves of Cass Maguire* (1966), *Crystal and Fox* (1968), *The Freedom of the City* (1973) and *Faith Healer* (1979). Many of these plays share common themes and concerns: the conflict between memory and objective reality, the relationship between the past and the present, the uncertainties and confusion of the individual soul, and the distance between appearance and reality. Perhaps the most pervasive and recurrent theme however is that of disappointment and failure.

Since the early seventies, Friel's writing has been influenced by political and social events in Northern Ireland, and by the resultant breakdown and disruption of northern society. His earlier plays tend to deal with the themes of disappointment and failure from the perspective of the individual. The later plays deal with them from the perspective of the community, and chart the process of disintegration in various northern communities.

In 1980 Brian Friel helped to establish the Field Day Theatre Company. Its first production was *Translations*, one of Friel's finest plays. *Translations* deals with the loss of the Irish language, the moment of cultural disintegration, when the Gaelic speaking order was replaced by an English speaking one. Friel, anxious to avoid a simplistic or pious attitude to this theme, satirises a nostalgic and sentimental attitude to Ireland's past in *The Communication Cord* (1982) the play which followed *Translations*. This latter parodies the attitude and feelings evoked in the earlier play.

In these two plays, as in nearly all his work, Friel explores the problem of identity and belonging, and the fragmented cultural inheritance which arises from our history as a colonised nation. In particular, Friel writes of Ulster, and more specifically, of Donegal where he now lives. He portrays the state of flux of his native place. In concentrating his gaze on a world that is local, even parochial, Friel expresses truths which have meaning for all.

In the 1990s Brian Friel has written a number of plays including *Fathers and Sons* and *A Month in the Country* which are adaptations of the Russian writer Turgenev's works. In 1990 he won international critical acclaim for his play *Dancing at Lughnasa* which recounts the lives of the five Mundy sisters at the time of the Festival of Lughnasa. This lively play, involving dancing and music, treats the themes of exile, hope and disintegration and shows Irish society under threat by modern values. The mythological undercurrents in *Dancing at Lughnasa* are followed up in *Wonderful Tennessee* (1993). This play, while expanding into the magical and mythological also returns to the familiar themes of exile, hope and dreaming found in *Philadelphia, Here I Come!* as, in rather Beckett-like fashion, three couples await a boatman to bring them across to the magical island, Oileán Draíochta.

Brian Friel's work is not particularly experimental. In formal terms, his plays fall within the conventions of modern realist drama, and his dramatic techniques are related to the two chief modes of realist drama, naturalism and expressionism. Within the conventions of realist theatre, Friel is an innovative dramatist, as *Philadelphia, Here I Come!* clearly demonstrates.

NATURALISM

Henrik Ibsen is often referred to as 'the father of modern drama'. Ibsen was concerned to give a true account of contemporary life in his dramatic art. He wished to portray the way in which ordinary people think, feel, speak and act. In his plays the details of the material world are rendered accurately and faithfully. The world as we perceive it is reproduced on stage. The stage conventions of naturalistic theatre influenced the production of plays in the Abbey Theatre especially during the 30s and 40s. Cottage interiors were reproduced with painstaking attention to detail. These cottage interiors, however, became rigidly conventional, and ultimately depicted a stage Irish version of the reality of contemporary life. The Abbey tradition is parodied in Friel's *The Communication Cord* (1982). The set of this play is reminiscent of the cottage interiors beloved of the Abbey. Repeatedly, however, the door of the cottage blows open and the interior is clouded in smoke from the turf fire. The *coup de grace* occurs in the final moment when the entire set collapses. Notwithstanding this gibe at the Abbey tradition, Friel's own work has been influenced by the traditions of naturalism. The O'Donnell house is carefully described in the stage directions. The accuracy or authenticity of the set is not an end in itself. The house is the narrow world within which Gar has to live. Seeing it, we recognise how difficult it is for Gar to survive within its confines.

Of course, naturalism is not solely or primarily concerned with external reality. It is more than a matter of furniture, objects, costumes and settings. In many naturalistic plays, we encounter characters who speak to one another but who fail to communicate, characters who are trapped within their material surroundings. *Philadelphia, Here I Come!* is obviously an example of this kind of drama. At the heart of the play is the failure of Gar and S.B. to speak to each other in a meaningful manner. The play is Friel's comment on a society that is habitually silent on matters of personal feelings.

THE HERO

In contrast to classical drama, the 'hero' of a realist play is hardly ever an extraordinary individual. The protagonists of realist dramas are characters with whom we can identify, people who are trapped in situations which we understand, and who are possessed of the same limited abilities and courage as ourselves. Gar O'Donnell is such a 'hero'. In classical theatre the moral order of the universe is often affirmed, and man's place within that order is asserted. Realist theatre works within no such perimeters. There is no order, no resolution beyond that which the protagonists can secure for themselves. Realist theatre is often a theatre of confusion and exposure, rarely of resolution. This is certainly true of *Philadelphia, Here I Come!* The final words spoken by S.B. in the play are 'I don't know either . . .' These words are also the final words uttered by Gar:

> Private: God, Boy, why do you have to leave? Why? Why?
> Public: I don't know. I — I — I don't know.

EXPRESSIONISM

'Expressionism', a term associated with the dramatist August Strindberg, refers to a style of drama which attempts to portray and define the inner forces and emotions of the characters on stage. These rarely find public expression and cannot be discerned externally or captured in naturalistic terms. Expressionism goes beyond the conventions of naturalist theatre in portraying the consciousness of the characters trapped in the rooms of naturalist drama. Expressionism is a development of realist theatre. Its aim is to give a true representation of life and a true representation of human psychology. The emphasis on the psychology of the individual and his/her states of consciousness introduces an unpredictable and energetic element into the drama that is often lacking in naturalistic theatre. Arthur Miller's *Death of a Salesman* is a case in point. This irrational and unpredictable element overcomes the tedium that can creep into a theatre solely concerned with external reality. Truthful and authentic dialogue is not necessarily entertaining dialogue. The public communication between

Gar and S.B., for example, is singularly uninteresting. It is thrown into comic relief by the humorous and sometimes acerbic commentary of Private:

> . . . But where was I? Oh, yes — our little talk — I'm beginning to wonder, Screwballs — I suspect — I'm afraid — *(in a rush, ashamed)* — I think I'm a sex-maniac! (p. 42)

The comic effect is achieved here by employing the most interesting expressionistic technique in the play, that of having two actors play the part of Gar.

DUAL PERSONALITY

The device of having two actors portray the public and private sides of Gar's personality serves many dramatic purposes. There is obvious comic potential in having a character on stage who is visible to the audience, but who does not 'exist' in the world of the drama. Many 'B' movies of the 40s and 50s make use of a similar technique with great comic effect. *The Ghost and Mrs Muir* is a well known example of this kind of light comedy. The very presence of the 'ghost' character brings a sense of playfulness into the situation and undermines the seriousness with which actions can be viewed. The fact that Private stands at the table between S.B. and the Canon as they play draughts makes the situation seem somehow ridiculous. His commentary is both funny and disturbing:

> Canon battling tooth and nail for another half-penny; Screwballs fighting valiantly to retain his trousers! Gripped in mortal combat! County Councillor versus Canon! Screwballs versus Canonballs. *(Stares intently at them.)* Hi, kids! Having fun, kids? *(Gets to his feet, leans his elbow on the table, and talks confidentially into their faces.)* Any chance of a game, huh? Tell me, boys, strictly between ourselves, will you miss me? You will? You really will? (p. 95)

The commentary continues in this vein for a short time, and then the tone and tenor of Private's remarks change and the mood of the play becomes darker:

> there's an affinity between Screwballs and me that no one,
> literally, no one could understand — except you, Canon
> *(deadly serious),* because you're warm and kind and soft and
> sympathetic — all things to all men — because you could
> translate all this loneliness, this groping, this dreadful bloody
> buffoonery into Christian terms that will make life bearable
> for us all. (p. 96)

In many respects, it is the 'character' of Private who controls and
directs the varying moods of the play.

The exchanges between Private and Public are another source of
hilarity in *Philadelphia.* The frantic interchanges, and the disparaging and
iconaclastic attitude of Private to almost every subject provide moments of
high comedy. The humour is frequently coarse, juvenile and wildly
exaggerated, reflecting the essential immaturity of Gar:

> And you know, too, that in his spare time he travels for
> maternity corsets; and that he's a double spy for the Knights
> and the Masons; and that he takes pornographic photographs
> of Mrs D. and sends them anonymously to reverend mothers.
> (p. 35)

The comedy derived from the technique of the dual personality reflects
Friel's attitude to the theatre. Undoubtedly, his intent and concerns are
serious, but this does not preclude him from entertaining his audience. He
regards theatre as a popular art-form: ' "serious" theatre will soon find that it
can't get a foothold on Broadway at all . . . And this, I think, is disastrous,
because it is an extension of the fallacy that important things must be
solemn, and because something is light-hearted it just can't be serious. I don't
have to refute this to you. But I would like to remind you that theatre is, by
definition, a *popular* art form. Euripides wrote for an audience of ten
thousand; and in the jargon of *Variety,* if that isn't boffo, what in the name of
God is?' *(The Theatre of Hope and Despair).* The exchanges of Private and
Public are reminiscent of a comic routine from the days of the variety hall.
This variety hall atmosphere is further conveyed in the extensive use of
music and song in the play, and the energetic movements of Private on stage.

The technique of the dual personality has, in addition to providing a
playful element, a serious objective. It is a way of dramatising the
psychological notion of ego and id. The device demonstrates the vast
difference between the spoken and the unspoken self. It reveals how little of

what moves or engages the individual is open to public perception. A dominant theme of *Philadelphia, Here I Come!* is the failure of characters to give voice to their inner selves. This is especially true of S.B. and Gar.

The dual personality technique allows Friel to express in a dramatic way the aggressiveness of the id and the force of many of the emotions suppressed by the individual. At all times in the play Friel suggests something of the richness and fullness of the inner life of the individual. The presence of Private on stage raises the question of the hidden thoughts and emotions of the other characters, especially of S.B. Does he, like Gar, possess a rich and expressive inner voice that fails to find public utterance? This is a question that Gar himself poses: 'God — maybe — Screwballs — behind those dead eyes and that flat face are there memories of precious moments in the past? My God, have I been unfair to you?' (p. 89).

FLASHBACK

In classical drama, the unities of time, place and action prescribed by Aristotle in his *Poetics* are normally observed. The structure of a classical tragedy tends towards the formula of exposition, conflict and resolution. The exposition introduces the characters and the seeds of the conflict; the second movement traces the conflict to its moment of crisis; the final movement presents the issue of the conflict and its resolution. It is a structure broadly adhered to by classical dramatists from Sophocles to Shakespeare.

The tragedy of these dramas is a necessary consequence of the actions of the hero. The emphasis on actions and consequences involves a sequential organisation of time in the drama — one thing leads to another. Macbeth's ambition, for example, leads to the murder of Duncan, which, in turn, leads to the ruin of Macbeth.

Generally, modern realist drama is less concerned with human action and its consequences than is classical theatre. *Philadelphia, Here I Come!* dramatises the failure of S.B. and Gar to take decisive action. Its main concern is to reveal the consciousness of the 'hero' and to portray, as truthfully as possible, his varying states of mind. Implicitly, it rejects the neat and logical structure imposed upon human affairs by classical dramatists. This is not to suggest that Shakespeare or Sophocles were not interested in portraying the minds of their heroes. In Shakespeare, there is a supreme interest in character, and the soliloquy is a device intended to make public the private thoughts and emotions of the character.

The concentration on the consciousness of Gar, in *Philadelphia, Here I Come!*, dictates the logic and pattern of the play. The passage of time towards the moment of departure is only one of the organising principles of *Philadelphia, Here I Come!* The inexorable march of time is indicated by many references to the clock and to time, as the evening unfolds, but within the time scale covered by the action of the play (seven hours), Gar's mind ranges over a period of twenty-five years. The imminence of his departure causes him to review the significant events which influenced his decision to quit Ballybeg. In particular his memory dwells on the interview with Senator Doogan, and the visit of his aunt Lizzy. These two incidents are re-enacted on stage, the action of the play shifting from the present to the past:

> (Three people have moved into the kitchen: Con Sweeney, Lizzy Sweeney, and Ben Burton. All three are in the fifty-five to sixty region. Burton is American, the Sweeneys Irish-American. Con Sweeney sits at the kitchen table with Ben Burton. Lizzy moves around in the centre of the kitchen. Public stands at the door of his bedroom. Private hovers around close to Public. p. 57)

Gar's memory and consciousness are the agencies through which this shift occurs. His memory deals with the past selectively and in a personal way, lingering on those events which have a subjective relevance. Thus the flashback scenes 'belong' to Gar's past in a special way. His inability to understand how each individual possesses the past in an uniquely private manner lies at the heart of his failure to communicate with S.B., in the final episode of the play.

STREAM OF CONSCIOUSNESS

The past is also made present through the flow of Gar's thoughts and the flow of his speech. Frequently Friel achieves a poetic effect by the use of a stream of consciousness technique. As a literary and theatrical device for revealing the inner thoughts of the protagonists, the stream of consciousness (or internal monologue, as it is sometimes called) has ample precedent. In Elizabethan drama, the soliloquy was a form of internal monologue frequently employed by Shakespeare. It allows him, for example, to reveal the disturbed state of Macbeth's mind on the night of Duncan's murder. In this century, the American playwright, Eugene O'Neill, 'rediscovered' the soliloquy. The most celebrated use of the convention however was by the Irish novelist, James Joyce. Joyce wished to imitate life and its processes as closely as possible through the medium of words. In developing the stream of consciousness technique, he learned from a number of developments in both science and art. He was impressed by the technique of montage in the making of motion pictures; he was aware of the impressionist movement, whose members interpreted the world from the perspective of the perceiving subject; he was undoubtedly influenced by the findings of psychoanalysis, and the idea of free association put forward by Jung and Freud.

As Joyce developed it, the stream of consciousness gave the impression of reproducing the thoughts of the individual just as they came into the mind. The technique employs only the most basic logical organisation, and sentences are reduced to their minimum form. Friel uses the technique on many occasions in the play. The character of Private is a dramatic embodiment of the internal monologue. In the final episode of the play, Madge speaks her thoughts as she tidies up before going to bed. The monologue is an exquisite example of the stream of consciousness. Madge's thoughts range from her own concerns to those of Gar. She thinks of Lizzy in America and her grandiose claims. Madge reveals both her scepticism and her worldly wisdom. The speech puts much of the previous action of the play into a wider perspective. It softens and lessens the feeling of crisis created by Gar. It is a speech written by a consummate dramatist.

Examining the Play

 ## A)   FOR DETAILED DISCUSSION

EPISODE 1

INTRODUCING GAR, MADGE AND S.B. (pp. 15-21)

1   What is our first impression of Gar O'Donnell?
2   Contrast Gar's way of talking with Madge's way of talking in this scene.
3   Comment on the significance of the opening exchanges between Private and Public.
4   Discuss the nature of Gar's fantasies, bearing in mind the fact that he is 25 years old.
5   What do we learn of Gar's attitude to (a) Ballybeg and (b) America?
6   Discuss Friel's use of comedy in the opening scene.
7   Compare Public and Private's reaction to S.B.
8   Does the first entrance of S.B. prepare us in any way for the relationship between him and his son?
9   How much of S.B.'s character is revealed in Friel's stage directions?

GAR'S FANTASIES CONTINUE (pp. 21-4)

1   What information about Gar's past is uncovered during the 'mock interview' fantasy?
2   What is the significance of Gar's use of the quotation from Edmund Burke's *Reflections on the Revolution in France*?
3   How does the switching from one voice to another dramatise Gar's conflict?
4   Comment on the subtle mixture of cultures displayed by Gar's fantasies in this sequence.
5   Public plays Mendelssohn's Violin Concerto. Is this choice of music in any way surprising?
6   Are Gar's fantasies in any way incongruous?

GAR'S MOTHER RECALLED (pp. 24-6)

1   What is the significance of the date on the faded newspaper which Gar finds in the suitcase?
2   Gar's recollections of the facts concerning his mother provide us with new and important information which is vital to the understanding of the play. Explain.
3   Gar's knowledge of his mother comes through Madge. What is the significance of this?
4   Gar's mother came from a place called Bailtefree. Is there any significance to the name of her home-place?
5   What do we learn of the relationship between S.B. and Maire in this scene?
6   Comment on Gar's use of the song *Philadelphia, Here I Come!*

KATE DOOGAN RECALLED (pp. 26-35)

1   How does Friel introduce the flashback technique?
2   Gar's emotional immaturity is clearly evident here. Discuss.
3   Compare Kate's and Gar's attitude to marriage.
4   What is the effect of Gar's revelation of the secret egg-money?
5   What do we learn about Senator Doogan's character in this scene?
6   Comment on the social contrast between the O'Donnells and the Doogans?
7   How does Gar react to the humiliating interview with Senator Doogan?
8   What is your attitude to Kate Doogan as her character is revealed in this scene?
9   'And when you think of a bugger like that, you want to get down on your knees and thank God for aul Screwballs.' What is the significance of this remark?

THE ROLE-PLAYING AND FANTASY (pp. 35-6)

1   Discuss the use of dialogue between Public and Private in this sequence.
2   The imagined dialogue between 'father' and 'son' in the first part of this sequence is in contrast to the conversations between S.B. and Gar in real life. Explain.
3   Comment on Gar's use of an American accent in the second part of this sequence.
4   The sexual innuendo of the conversation between Public and Private reveals something of Gar's character. Discuss.
5   Friel regards drama as a popular art. How is this reflected in Gar's fantasies and role-playing?

MADGE AND GAR (pp. 37-8)

1   What do we learn about Madge's character in this scene?
2   How does Gar demonstrate his love for Madge?
3   From the evidence of this scene, how would you describe the role of Madge in the O'Donnell household?

TEA-TIME AT O'DONNELLS' (pp. 38-43)

1   Private's parody of the gestures and speech of S.B. is a comic highlight in the play. Discuss.
2   Compare Public's attitude towards Madge in this scene with his attitude towards her in the previous scene.
3   If the audience had not a privileged view of Private, Gar would appear as banal and pedantic as his father. Discuss.
4   What is the significance of the shifting moods of Private's personality?
5   How would you describe Gar's suggestions for that 'one unpredictable remark'?
6   What is the effect of S.B.'s repetition of 'I didn't find as many about the year'?
7   Comment on Madge's interventions during this scene?
8   The lack of communication between father and son is the central tragedy of *Philadelphia*. Would you agree with this statement? Give reasons for your answer.

MASTER BOYLE'S VISIT (pp. 43-8)

1   What is the significance of S.B.'s hasty departure from the kitchen when Master Boyle enters?
2   Master Boyle is the antithesis of the responsible, respectable citizens of Ballybeg. Discuss.
3   What aspects of Boyle's character emerge during his visit?
4   Gar has an ambivalent attitude to Master Boyle. He describes him as being a 'sorry wreck . . . arrogant and pathetic'; yet he holds a certain affection for him. Discuss the dual aspect of Gar's attitude to Master Boyle.
5   Would you agree that the sequence in which Boyle embraces Gar is the emotional highlight of Episode l? Give reasons for your answer.
6   Discuss Gar's reaction to the embrace.
7   Compare Gar's mood in the opening scene with his mood at the close of Episode 1.
8   What does Madge's comment about Master Boyle reveal about her personality?

EPISODE 2

KEEPING UP THE SPIRITS (pp. 51-4)

1 Compare Gar's mood here with his mood in the opening sequence of the play.
2 How does Private try to prevent Public from getting swallowed up in sentimentality?
3 Comment on the use of the song *She Moved Through The Fair*.
4 How true is Private's remark that Gar wants to make himself 'bloody miserable'?

THE RETURNED EMIGRANTS (pp. 54-66)

1 What three marriages are brought into focus in this scene?
2 How might these marriages be said to repeat a pattern of failure and disappointment?
3 How would you describe Lizzy's attitude to Con?
4 What is her relationship to Ben Burton, and how is it revealed?
5 Why do you think Con accepts Lizzy's remarks with patience and resignation?
6 In what way is Ben Burton representative of America?
7 What is Lizzy's attitude to Ballybeg and to Madge?
8 In what sense can Lizzy and Madge be regarded as rivals?
9 What are the two major factors which influence Gar's decision to accept the invitation to America?

THE WORDS THAT HURT THE MOST (pp. 66-7)

1 Compare the conversation between Gar and Madge in this scene with previous conversations between them.
2 Would you agree that the tension heightens in the play throughout this scene?
3 What evidence is there that Madge is no longer optimistic that S.B. will say or do anything to demonstrate his affection for Gar?
4 How would you interpret Madge's outburst against S.B. at the end of this sequence?
5 What evidence is there that
   (a) Madge and
   (b) S.B. are upset by Gar's imminent departure for Philadelphia?
6 Does this sequence prepare us in any way for the entrance of 'the boys'?

THE VISIT OF 'THE BOYS' (pp. 68-76)

1 In *Philadelphia, Here I Come!* Friel's stage directions are a very important element. Discuss this statement with reference to the scene where 'the boys' visit Gar.

2   What do you learn about the character of Ned in this sequence?

3   What do Madge's comments reveal about her attitude to 'the boys'?

4   'The boys' embody the fantasy and role-playing already displayed by Private. Would you agree with this statement? Support your answer with references to the play.

5   In your own words, outline the reasons why 'the boys' refuse to talk about Gar's impending departure.

6   Ned and Tom exaggerate their version of past events. Give examples and explain in your own words why they do this.

7   The visit of 'the boys' is another example of lack of communication in the play. Discuss.

8   What is the significance of Ned's awkward parting gift to Gar?

9   Why does Gar encourage Joe to go and follow Ned and Tom?

10 How does Gar react to the knowledge that Madge invited 'the boys' to come and visit him?

11 In your own words, analyse Gar's speech beginning 'They're louts, ignorant bloody louts . . .'.

KATE'S VISIT (pp. 79-83)

1   What affect has Kate's visit on Gar?

2   Gar tells Kate that he will probably go to night-school in Philadelphia and 'do law or medicine or something'.
    (a) What is the significance of this remark?
    (b) Discuss Private's reaction to this remark?

3   In this scene, Private is the one who tries to calm Public. Discuss.

4   S.B.'s failure to communicate any sense of loss at Gar's departure is one of the central preoccupations of the play. Is there evidence here to support or refute this statement?

5   How do you react to Gar's pronouncement that S.B., the Canon, Master Boyle, and 'the boys' are all 'Asylum cases'?

6   Gar adopts the vocabulary of Ned and Master Boyle in this scene. Discuss the significance of this with examples from the text.

7   Do you think Gar is sincere when he says that he hates Ballybeg 'and every stone, and every rock, and every piece of heather around it!'?

8   What do we learn of Kate's character from this scene and from the previous flashback sequence (pp. 26-35)?

9   After Kate's departure, Gar's mood changes. Comment on Gar's fluctuating moods in this sequence.

10 Discuss Friel's use of the stream of consciousness technique with particular reference to Private's last speech in this scene.

EPISODE 3 — PART 1

INCANTATION AND REVERIE (pp. 87-91)

1   The picture Private presents of Gar's future is a romantic version of S.B.'s life. Would you agree or disagree with this statement? Support your answer with reference to the text.
2   Gar's recollection of the fishing trip with his father is expressed in some of the most poetic and romantic language in the play. Discuss.
3   Is there any evidence here that time is running out for Gar?
4   Gar can see with great clarity the self-delusions of 'the boys', but he is blind to his own. Discuss.
5   Is there a contrast between the tone and content of Gar's remarks to his father?

CANON O'BYRNE'S VISIT (pp. 91-9)

1   What do we learn of Canon O'Byrne's character from this scene?
2   Would you agree that the Canon and S.B. are conspirators in the silence surrounding Gar's exile?
3   Discuss the part played by Madge in this scene.
4   The 'affinity' between the Canon and S.B. is highlighted by the interwoven pattern of their language. Discuss with reference to the text.
5   Comment on the relationship between Gar and Madge, as revealed here.
6   Compare this sequence with the tea-time sequence, paying particular attention to the role of Private, and the varying moods he displays.
7   Discuss the comic element here.
8   What is the significance of Public playing Mendelssohn's record?

EPISODE 3 — PART 2

GAR AND S.B. (pp. 100-6)

1   In this scene father and son are engaged in the same activity — collecting memories and images from the past. Discuss with references from the text.
2   (a) What is the significance of S.B.'s remark: 'Sure you know I never take a second cup'?
    (b) Compare how this remark affects Gar in this scene and in the tea-time scene.

3   Comment on S.B.'s advice to Gar about where he should sit on the plane.

4   How does Gar react when he discovers that his father has no recollection of the fishing trip?

5   With particular reference to this scene, discuss the theory that memory is illusive and defective in *Philadelphia, Here I Come!*

6   Is S.B. embarrassed to be found in the kitchen in the small hours of the morning?

7   S.B. searches out the truth of Gar's memories. What does this tell us of his character?

8   Do you think that Gar is in any way unfair to S.B. in this scene?

A BOY IN A SAILOR-SUIT (pp 106-8)

1   What is the source of Madge's disappointment in this scene?

2   Do you think that S.B. is in any way blameworthy for failing to perceive her disappointment?

3   In what sense does S.B.'s recollection of the sailor-suit episode answer Gar's earlier questioning, 'God — maybe Screwballs — behind those dead eyes and that flat face are there memories of precious moments in the past?'

4   Does this scene alter your impression of the character of S.B.?

5   What is the dramatic effect of the repetition of the phrase 'I don't know'?

FINALE (pp 108-10)

1   What is the effect of Madge's monologue on the mood of the play?

2   How, if at all, does Madge bring a new sense of perspective to Gar's anguish?

3   What elements of Madge's character are most clearly evident in her monologue?

4   Do you agree with Madge's remark that Gar will turn out 'just the same' as his father?

5   Is there any significance in the form of Madge's address to Gar: 'I'm just tired, son. Very tired'?

6   Is there any self-deception in Private's observation: 'this is a film you'll run over and over again — Madge Going to Bed On My Last Night At Home . . .'?

7   Why might it be argued that we leave Gar as we find him?

8   How valid is the argument that *Philadelphia, Here I Come!* deals with nothing more profound than a young man who is fearful of leaving home for the first time?

B) FOR GENERAL DISCUSSION

1 *Philadelphia, Here I Come!* is a study of an unsettled young man in the process of growing up.

2 The drama is a superb study of the torments and gyrations of the adolescent mind in the throes of maturing.

3 The father/son relationship dominates the play.

4 Private does much more than laugh when the hero cries and cry when he laughs.

5 Gar's part dominates but does not drown out the others.

6 The language of *Philadelphia, Here I Come!* is naturalistic and authentic.

7 The play as a statement about Ireland.

8 Life in America may be as claustrophic for Gar as life in Ballybeg.

9 The general pattern of shifting moods in the play.

10 The function of the comic exchanges in the play.

11 Discuss the relationship between the two Gars.

12 Did young Gareth O'Donnell really emigrate from the old country?

13 The logic of the play is not in plot contrivance or 'what-happens-next', but in its delicate montage of past and present experience and feeling.

14 The playwright's first function is to entertain . . . to participate in lavish and luxurious goings-on!

15 Ultimately, the play is talking in the broadest terms about estrangement, loneliness, and human hopes of understanding and intimacy.

16. Buffoonery causes misunderstanding and prevents meaningful contact with others, except at a superficial level, because it disguises true feelings. Discuss in relation to *Philadelphia, Here I Come!*

17 In the course of the play, the comic and exuberant clowning gives way to a more hardened form of role-playing.

18 Gar does not act the clown, he *is* the clown in the original sense of the word.

19 The use of a dual protagonist — Public and Private — may at first glance suggest a split personality or schizophrenia.

20 Although they may occasionally taunt, curse or contradict one another, Public and Private basically are not at odds with each other.

21 Gar and S.B. — 'as like as two peas'?

22 It is not difficult to imagine how age and further disappointment may take the humour and the spirit out of Gar altogether and leave him a taciturn man.

23 Discuss the role of music and song in the play.

24 The play as a social commentary on life in Ireland today.

Critical Comment

The following selection of critical opinions has been chosen to illustrate significant aspects of *Philadelphia, Here I Come!*

1 Gar's isolation: *'Philadelphia, Here I Come!* concerns the isolation of those who cannot convey their true feelings to each other — exemplified here as failure of communication among the members of a small-town family. Gar O'Donnell, offered the alternative of emigration to the USA or unchallenging work in his father's store, is constitutionally unable to respond openly to the emotions which his decision to emigrate stir in his own mind, and in the minds of his intractable father, his aunt Lizzie, his girlfriend, his mates, and the housekeeper Madge who is the all-understanding maternal figure. The technical device of introducing two actors to portray Gar and his *alter ego* — between whom there are pithy exchanges of dialogue — gives the play additional psychological point, most subtly when Gar Private's 'unheard' comments contradict the actual remarks of Gar Public. The brisk country humour of the dialogue tellingly underscores the anguish of unexpressed personal dislocation.'

C. Fitz-Simon

2 Gar, the exile: 'Gar O'Donnell is, in many ways, a recognizably modern case of alienation. He has all the narcissism that goes with the condition of being driven back in upon the resources of the self. But Friel is so specific in his evocation of the conditions of Irish life, so insistent in the deep-rooted sense of inherited failure, that the play has the freshness of a revelation rather than the routine characteristics of a well-known situation. Since the beginning of this century, Irish drama has been heavily populated by people for whom vagrancy and exile have become inescapable conditions about which they can do nothing but talk, endlessly and eloquently and usually to themselves. The tramps of Yeats and Synge and Beckett, the stationless slum dwellers of O'Casey or Behan, bear a striking family resemblance to Friel's exiles.'

Seamus Deane

3 A spiritual leavetaking: 'Gareth must also fight a subtler kind of slavery. Before he can enter the jet, he must wrench himself from the womb of place. To be reborn, he must be unborn. He must blot out the streets and scents of Ballybeg. He must stop his ears against the voices of friends and their loutish camaraderie. He must stiffen in the embrace of the drunken schoolmaster, a surrogate father who has fed Gareth's blind yearnings as surely as his true father has starved his spirit. And he must face the vision of what he may become, in the person of a blowsy ginned-up Irish-American aunt who is making his exodus to America possible.'

Time review

4 Gar's feelings for Ballybeg: 'He is often in the clutch of sad reflections about his life in Ballybeg. Over the years, he has only once had some sort of emotional communication with his dour widowed father, and he has lost all chance of marrying his sweetheart because he became tongue-tied when he had an opportunity to claim her. But though he is oppressed by the monotony of Ballybeg — the irksome labor in his father's store, the empty chatter about imagined sexual conquests by his loutish friends, the dreary colloquies between his father and the local canon over a checker-board, the disintegration before his eyes of a schoolteacher he respected — he is nevertheless not without affection for the place, and not without fear for his welfare in Philadelphia, where he will have to live under the roof of a frowsty, bibulous aunt'.

The New Yorker review

5 Gar, growing up: *'Philadelphia, Here I Come!* is a play about a young man in the painful process of growing up. Taciturn and tongue-tied in the presence of his elders, frustrated and discontented in the company of his peers, disappointed in love through his own inadequacy, Gar nevertheless starts with an essentially youthful, bright and cynical alter ego. Gar's humor and resiliency begin to desert him in the course of the drama. The uncertain escape to Philadelphia, to the overwhelming and smothering motherliness of his vulgar Aunt Lizzie, offers no satisfactory alternative, and the play ends on a subdued note of disappointment, uncertainty, indecision and doubt. Gar lacks security, self-confidence, and inner freedom, and hides his instability behind a number of different masks that vary in form but not in function. The drama is a superb study of the torments and gyrations of the adolescent mind in the throes of maturing. Gar's future development as an adult is left open, as uncertain as the last words of the play: "I don't know. I — I — I don't know".'

E. H. Winkler

6 Gar's personality: 'The two major features of Gar's personality are, on the one hand, discontent with his present life and its future perspectives, together with a desire to escape from its humdrum routine; and on the other hand, a deep-seated longing for psychological security, for emotional roots. Gar is torn between these two extremes, and this conflict finds an outlet both in clowning and in fantasy role-playing.'

E. H. Winkler

7 Gar and S.B.: ' "Old Screwballs," as Gareth refers to him, is clench-lipped, word-shy, and sclerotically set in his ways. An evening with him is an unaltering ritual of despair: one cup of tea (never two), a game of checkers with the canon, a grunt of shoptalk. Gareth's father puts on his glasses to see the paper, never his son. Yet there is a kind of love between the two, all the more painful for being inarticulate. The words that hurt the most on this final evening together are the words that are not said.'

Time review

8 Gar's future: 'Given the action of the play, it is not difficult to imagine how age and further disappointment may take the humor and the spirit out of Gar altogether and leave him a taciturn man, like his father, burying his feelings behind an almost impenetrable wall of habit and convention.'

E. H. Winkler

9 'The boys': 'Their endless reminiscence of imaginary seductions conceals a reality of futile street wanderings, of cold, of locked doors, and of drawn blinds.'

D. E. S. Maxwell

10 Dual personality technique: 'Brian Friel is a conventional dramatist in that he generally employs a linear plot. He does, however, make some startling experiments with that form: the physically-split personality of Gar O'Donnell, which affects the structure of *Philadelphia, Here I Come!* is a case in point. Such effects surprise the audience into a different kind of awareness, and cause its members to listen more closely.'

C. Fitz-Simon

11 Public and Private: 'The most striking structural peculiarity of *Philadelphia, Here I Come!,* the use of a dual protagonist — Public and Private — may at first glance suggest a split personality or schizophrenia. But, very early in the play, it becomes obvious that this is not Friel's real intention in creating the two Gars. Although they may occasionally taunt, curse or contradict one another, Public and Private basically are not at odds with each other. Both share the same fantasies and dreams and both play together in scenes of extended imagination. In the light of the psychologically insecure character, then, it is not the dual protagonists as such which interest us, but rather the talent of both Public and Private Gar for mimicry, their tendency to clown, fool about and play roles, since this indicates an immature mind.'

E. H. Winkler

12 Gar Private: 'This palpable alter ego, invisible to the other characters, acts as a jazzy Greek chorus, a human pep pill, and a court jester. He laughs when the hero cries and cries when the hero laughs — an alert, ironic, ever-present border guard to keep self-pity from invading pity.'

Time review

13 The power of memory: 'The play expresses a tender awareness of how memory distils events, with the evening's nicest irony being that the uncommunicative father remembers his son through one past incident, while the lonely young man remembers his father through a different one. But the tragic fact is that neither can recall the other's incident.'

Saturday Review

14 Gar's buffoonery: 'It not only forms a protective shield behind which he can hide to lessen and deaden pain and disappointment, buffoonery also actually causes misunderstanding and prevents meaningful contact with others, except at a superficial level, because it disguises true feelings.'

E. H. Winkler

15 Grimness and the possibility of joy: 'The play is a statement first of all, and necessarily, about particular people in a particular grouping. More generally it is a statement about Ireland, the Ireland of religious and sexual frigidity, of overbearing old age, of joyless, close-mouthed rural puritanism; and of their opposites. The play's humor reflects them and is often, understandably, savage enough. Gar likes Madge; she is also, callously, "aul' fluke-feet."'

D. E. S. Maxwell

16 An Irish, yet universal play: 'Ultimately, the play is talking in the broadest terms about estrangement, loneliness, and human hopes of understanding and intimacy. Unequivocally "Irish," *Philadelphia* traverses its regional boundaries.'

D. E. S. Maxwell

The following general comments by Brian Friel illustrate some of his preoccupations as a dramatist, preoccupations which have a particular relevance to *Philadelphia, Here I Come!*

1 Alienation and conflict: '"Man", says Lucky in *Waiting For Godot*, "in brief in spite of the strides of alimentation and defecation wastes and pines wastes and pines." And since man's span of life is all that he has, with nothing ultimate to inspire or support him, since God is dead and with Him the tragic hero, the only concern of the modern dramatist is man in society, in conflict with community, government, academy, church, family — and essentially in conflict with himself.'

2 The rulers and the rest: 'The world, according to the dramatists, is divided into two categories. There are the rulers — the establishment — who pretend to believe in a traditional social structure that is Christian in origin, that is now seen to be false, but which they still pretend to believe in in order to give them the authority they require. And there are simply the rest — individuals, isolated, separated, sick and disillusioned with their inheritance, existing in the void created by their rejection, waiting without hope for a new social structure that will give a meaning to their lives. For a time it looked as if Communism — or even what we vaguely call the Left — might be the new messiah. But that, too, has failed. Everything has failed — politics, art, science, religion, philosophy. Man wastes and pines wastes and pines.'

3 The function of the dramatist: 'The answer to these questions is that dramatists have no solutions. Furthermore, it is not their function to give answers. They are not marriage counsellors, nor father confessors, nor politicians, nor economists. What function have they, then? They have this function: they are vitally, persistently, and determinedly concerned with one man's insignificant place in the here-and-now world. They have the function to portray that one man's frustrations and hopes and anguishes and joys and miseries and pleasures with all the precision and accuracy and truth that they know; and by so doing help to make a community of individuals. They have this function — their supreme function, I think, and one they share with all groping, trumpeting artists everywhere and at all times, and it is this: that they recognise with great clarity the conflict between the world of the flesh and the world of the spirit, or if you dislike the terms, the world of the physical and the world of the cerebral. And when they depict in mean, gruesome detail only one portion of our existence, perhaps in this generation the dominant portion, they are crying out for recognition of the existence of something less ignoble, something more worthy. They are asking us to recognise that even in confusion and disillusion, strength and courage can exist, and that out of them can come a redemption of the human spirit.'

4 The purpose of drama: 'Anger is a theatrical technique. The theatre is altogether so different from a short story anyhow. You get a group of people sitting in an audience and they aren't individual thinking people any longer once they're in an audience. They are a corporate group who act in the same way as a mob reacts — react emotionally and spontaneously. Now you can move these people by making them angry. You can make them sympathetic. You can make them laugh. You can make them cry. You can do all these things. And this emotional reaction doesn't live very long, doesn't last very long; I mean, they will not storm out of a theatre and pull down a Government. Or they will not storm out of a theatre and build homes for people that haven't got houses. But there is always the chance that a few people will retain a certain amount of the spontaneous reaction that they experienced within the theatre building and that they will think about this when they come outside. And perhaps they may do something. But this is not the end purpose. The end purpose is to move them, and you will move them, in a theatre anyhow, not through their head but through their heart. Brendan Behan used to say that you keep the people laughing in a theatre for five minutes and then in the sixth minute, when they're helpless laughing, you plug your message, if you want to plug a message.'

Select Bibliography

STAGE PLAYS

Philadelphia, Here I Come!, London, Faber & Faber, 1965; New York, Farrar, Straus & Giroux, 1966

The Loves of Cass McGuire, London, Samuel French, 1966; London, Faber & Faber, 1967; New York, Farrar, Straus & Giroux, 1967

Lovers, New York, Farrar, Straus & Giroux, 1968; London, Faber & Faber, 1969

Crystal and Fox, London, Faber & Faber, 1970; New York, Farrar, Straus & Giroux, 1970 (in *Two Plays*)

The Mundy Scheme, London, Samuel French, 1970; New York, Farrar, Straus & Giroux, 1970 (in *Two Plays*)

The Gentle Island, London, Davis Poynter, 1973

The Freedom of the City, London, Faber & Faber, 1974; New York, Samuel French, 1974

The Enemy Within, Newark, Delaware, Proscenium Press, 1975; Dublin, Gallery Press, 1979

Living Quarters, London, Faber & Faber, 1978

Volunteers, London, Faber & Faber, 1979

Faith Healer, London, Faber & Faber, 1980; New York, Samuel French, 1980

Aristocrats, Dublin, Gallery Press, 1980; London, Faber & Faber, 1984

Translations, Faber & Faber, 1981; New York, Samuel French, 1981

The Three Sisters (translated from Chekhov), Dublin, Gallery Press, 1981

The Communication Cord, London, Faber & Faber, 1983

Selected Plays of Brian Friel (with Introduction by Seamus Deane), London, Faber & Faber, 1984

Fathers and Sons, London, Faber & Faber, 1987

Making History, London, Faber & Faber, 1989

The London Vertigo, Meath, Gallery Press, 1990

Dancing at Lughnasa, London, Faber & Faber, 1990

A Month in the Country, Meath, Gallery Press, 1992

Wonderful Tennessee, Meath, Gallery Press, 1993

SHORT-STORY COLLECTIONS

The Saucer of Larks, London, Gollancz, 1962; Garden City, NY, Doubleday, 1962

The Gold in the Sea, London, Gollancz, 1966; Garden City, NY, Doubleday, 1966

Selected Stories, Dublin, Gallery Press, 1970; published as *The Diviner: The Best Stories of Brian Friel,* Dublin, O'Brien Press, 1982; London, Allison & Busby, 1982

CONTRIBUTION TO PERIODICALS

The Theatre of Hope and Despair (text of lecture), *Everyman* (Benburb, Co. Tyrone), no. 1, 1968

BIOGRAPHY

Brian Friel, Desmond E. S. Maxwell, Lewisburg, Pa, Bucknell University Press, 1973

CRITICISM

A Critical History of Modern Irish Drama 1891-1980, D. E. S. Maxwell, Cambridge University Press, 1984

The Irish Theatre, Christopher Fitz-Simon, London, Thames and Hudson Ltd., 1983

Books and Authors: Eejitin' About: Adolescence in Friel and Keane, Elizabeth Hale Winkler, (Article in) Eire 16(3) pp. 138-144,1981